TIDYING UP

EA FUQUA & MEG DELONG

Founders and Owners of
THE TIDY HOME NASHVILLE

As you read through the book, be sure to visit our website and socials to learn more and to also find shopping lists for the items we've recommended.

www.thetidyhomenashville.com
@thetidyhomenashville

Tidying Up

Copyright © 2025 Ea Fuqua and Meg DeLong

All rights reserved. No portion of this book may be reproduced, stored in a retrieval system, or transmitted in any form or by any means—electronic, mechanical, photocopy, recording, scanning, or other—except for brief quotations in critical reviews or articles, without the prior written permission of the publisher.

Published by Harper Celebrate, an imprint of HarperCollins Focus LLC.

The authors are represented by Alive Literary Agency, www.aliveliterary.com.

Any internet addresses (websites, blogs, etc.) in this book are offered as a resource. They are not intended in any way to be or imply an endorsement by HarperCollins Focus LLC, nor does HarperCollins Focus LLC vouch for the content of these sites for the life of this book.

Cover design by Kathy Mitchell
Interior design by Kristen Sasamoto
Photo courtesy of authors (page 209).

ISBN 978-1-4002-5322-7 (HC)
ISBN 978-1-4002-5321-0 (ebook)
ISBN 978-1-4002-5319-7 (audio)

Printed in Malaysia

25 26 27 28 29 OFF 5 4 3 2 1

To our Mom and Dad

You taught us to embrace the unknown, to take risks, and not to fear new things. Among the many gifts you've given us, you instilled in us the art of keeping a home both tidy and inviting. We always had the house all our friends wanted to be at, all the slumber parties and balloon fights—some of our favorite memories. But the greatest gift of all was each other—a sister to navigate life with. Thank you for being our greatest cheerleaders. We love you both so much!

CONTENTS

INTRODUCTION

Hi! Thank you for meeting us here! We're Ea and Meg, two sisters with two different personalities, both of whom have found meaning, purpose, and most profoundly, peace through the process of tidying up our homes. Our journey into home organization began in 2019 out of necessity. We both were barely surviving our days, feeling stressed out and overwhelmed. At that time, one of us had a new baby while the other had a growing family and worked from home. We constantly felt frustrated, guilty, and insecure. With anxiety mounting, we were desperately grasping for a hint of normalcy and predictability. But what we craved more than a clean home with efficient systems was a sense of order *inside ourselves.*

Both of us found that the process of tidying up our homes helped us manage the sense of unease that was affecting us both mentally and physically. The goal was never to have a perfectly curated home, one enviable by other women or worthy of a photo shoot. We simply wanted peace and calm. What we wanted—and what we *needed*—was to feel better. What a relief it was to our minds and bodies when we learned how much outer order created inner calm.

And that's exactly what we found.

We now work with clients all over the country, helping people in all walks of life tackle their clutter and create organization. We create order out of chaos in homes that range from super small apartments to literal mansions. We help our clients come up with sustainable systems for their unique spaces. While the particular solutions are specific to each client, the underlying principles stay the same. And more than marveling at how pretty everything looks afterward, we absolutely love doing this work because of how our clients *feel* afterward. They experience that same peace and purpose that both of us experienced when we finally tackled the clutter in our own homes.

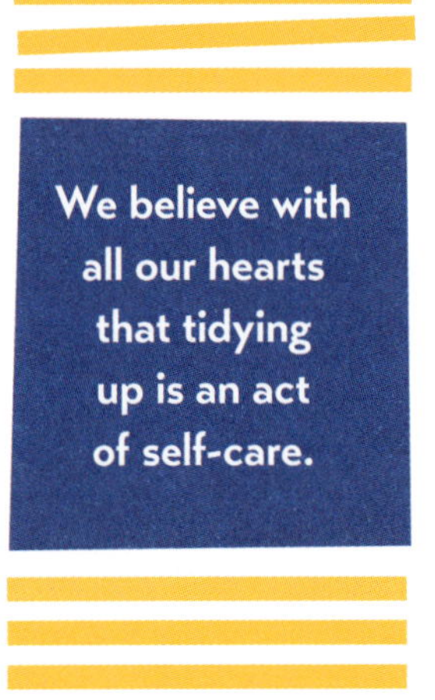

This sense of peace and purpose is exactly what we want for you too. Our goal in these pages is to empower you to believe you *can* create order in your home. And to discover that when you do, you *will* feel better.

For some readers, every area of the home needs a lot of help and attention, and for others, perhaps only some tweaks here and there are needed. Maybe your bedroom is pristine but the kitchen is a chronic mess. Maybe you have all your photos organized but your paperwork is out of control. Maybe you were always a person with a place for everything until the kids came along or the job became more demanding. No matter your starting point, we believe there's something for everyone in these pages.

Fundamentally, we believe with all our hearts that tidying up is an act of self-care and can improve your mental health. We've seen it happen firsthand. We love watching the anxiety and confusion fade away when we employ a well-planned decluttering system. We love experiencing a well-functioning home and the subsequent improved relationships with our friends and family. And we love seeing the meaningful transformations that happen in our clients' lives as a result.

A tidy life is the possibility that lies ahead for you. We feel so strongly that you are worthy of the time and energy it takes to tidy up your home. You deserve to feel good in the space where you spend so much of your time. You deserve calm . . . peace . . . room to breathe. You deserve time and space to play with your kids without worrying about all the toys everywhere, because you'll know they all have their own places to go. You deserve the opportunity to sit down on the couch with your partner or friends or family and truly, deeply relax. Doesn't that sound amazing? Because when you are calm, at peace, and centered (instead of constantly flustered, frazzled, and burnt out), you can be present to the wonderful life

you have and enjoy the people you share it with.

For those who live with other people, whether family or otherwise, tidying up the home will help everyone else too. When you involve them in the process, they also learn how to keep the home streamlined and efficient—allowing you to remain calm and centered. The effects on your relationships can be profound. There's more room to laugh, to connect, and to simply *be* with the people you love and enjoy the most. Tidying goes well beyond figuring out organizational systems; it's a way of life that brings hope and joy to everyone.

At the core of our work, we believe you deserve to feel good in your home.

HOW TO READ THIS BOOK

Some of you (hello, firstborns) will read this book in order, chapter by chapter. Others are more inclined to jump into the chapters that interest you most—perhaps diving in to the sections that address the areas of your home that need the most help. Some will read a chapter, put the book down, and tackle that space. And others of you will finish the last page before you start tidying up.

However you decide to read this book and get started, just know this: It all works!

That said, we have written the chapters in an order that we believe makes sense for how to tidy up an entire home in a way that's achievable and sustainable. And while the chapters do build on one another, each one stands on its own.

Since we have written this book together, most often we'll talk about our lives in general and the systems we created, so we might use "we" at times. And sometimes one of us will share a personal experience. For ease of reading, and because we're a package deal, we've decided to use the pronoun "I" but not identify which one of us is speaking (or writing) each time, especially since we both agree with the overall messages and methods.

SIX IMPORTANT THINGS TO KNOW BEFORE WE START

1. More square footage isn't the answer. Really, it's not. You live where you live, and until you move, this is the space you have. So let's make it work—and make it work well. We've organized small Brooklyn apartments and enormous Nashville mansions. Each unique space, whatever the square footage, requires a combination of creativity and efficiency. No matter the size of your home, there's a solution.
2. Take your time. Regardless of your energy level, we invite you to view organizing your home as an act of self-care.

Tidying your space is a way to calm and settle your nervous system.[1] This process can go as slow or fast as you want. Remember: *There is no deadline.*

3. **You have a choice and get to set your own priorities.** You get to choose where in your home to start. You get to decide what goes and what stays. We are not here to pressure you. But please keep in mind that whatever you hold on to in one part of your home means you'll likely have to compensate by eliminating something else from another part. We'll help you through this; don't worry.
4. **It's a group effort.** If you live with other people, it's important to communicate about the process of tidying up, especially as you begin. Whether you call a family meeting, have a heart-to-heart with your spouse, or simply have a conversation at the dinner table, you want your family to be on board and play their part. Tell them what tidying up means to you, what your goals are for the home, and how it can help all of you. Tidying up is a group effort.
5. **Set an example.** This one is for the parents out there (so if that's not you, you can skip ahead). As parents, whatever habits and behaviors we prioritize and model, our kids will pick up on. *If they have a mess, it's okay for me to have one too.* We always want better for our kiddos than for ourselves, so keeping our spaces tidy will model the benefits—mentally, emotionally, and financially—to our littles and offer them strategies to carry into adulthood. Ideally, these behaviors and habits become second nature.

6. **Your goal is peace.** We want to help save both your sanity and money through this process. If any of our tips and products feel like overkill or don't work for your home or budget, feel free to skip to the next section with our blessing. At the heart of what we do, we want you to feel at peace in your home—and that includes peace in the process of getting there.

As we begin, give yourself space, time, and maybe some headphones (or a glass of wine) and start small. We know you can do this! Take one area at a time and get to work. There's no timeline. But you might be surprised by how freeing it is (and dare we say fun?) to keep going once you've started. Although we offer a lot of tips and tricks, we want so much more for you than a tidy closet or laundry room. This book is a pathway to simplicity and sustainability, one that we believe will truly change your life.

And as you read through the book, be sure to visit our website and socials to learn more about the products we've recommended.

As you read through the book, be sure to visit our website and socials to learn more and to also find shopping lists for the items we've recommended.

www.thetidyhomenashville.com
@thetidyhomenashville

Chapter One

TIDYING UP YOUR CLEANING SUPPLIES

We'd like to start our tidying-up journey together with a space that tends to have less emotional weight than some of the others—a space that will get you on the right track as you move forward with the rest of your home. Our first task is to tackle the laundry room, utility room, or wherever you store your cleaning supplies. Whether you have a full laundry room or simply a few shelves in a closet, organizing this space is a perfect starting point because it's so central to the rest of what you're going to do throughout the tidying-up process. When we have the right systems in place, it's amazing how good this new sense of control can make us feel.

When we say "the right" or "a great" system, what we really mean is a plan that is efficient and functional for the layout of *your* home. In newer homes, laundry rooms are typically on the same level as the kitchen, living room, or entryways. But some homes have an upstairs laundry, and many older homes often have them in the basement. No matter your situation, the key to a great laundry room is establishing systems that everyone can understand. A working laundry room setup saves time, money, and sanity when everything is easily accessible. But this doesn't benefit you alone; life feels a bit easier when everyone else in the home knows where the extra hand soap lives too!

SYSTEM SUCCESS

When laid out poorly, laundry rooms can easily become a source of stress and overwhelm. Sometimes just walking by them can stir up feelings of judgment. *These piles of laundry aren't going to fold themselves!* When it's unclear what's even clean or dirty anymore, these dizzying spaces become hidden traps for shame and anxiety. And we get it—whether you live in a four-hundred-square-foot apartment or a four-thousand-square-foot ranch home, figuring out a system that works for you can be tricky and feel insurmountable.

But once you unlock this room's organization, every other room's organizational success will follow suit. With just a few systems in place, you can turn overwhelm into peace and clutter into clarity.

CLUTTER IS THE KRYPTONITE OF MOTIVATION

Laundry rooms can quickly become a catchall for almost everything—namely, all the projects you're tempted to put off. Are guests coming over and piles of laundry are all over the floor? Shove them back in the laundry room! Need to glue a piece of a toy back together for your kiddo? Throw it in the laundry room till you can get to it. Need to sew on a button? Laundry room! *We all do this.* But think about how much all that clutter negatively affects your motivation.

A direct correlation exists between how much visual clutter there is in a laundry room and how much motivation a person has to do the laundry in a timely manner—let alone clean the rest of the house. It's not fun standing on a pile of dirty laundry while looking for the window cleaner. We want to help you focus on small changes in this space so you can transform it from a room you avoid to one that supports you and helps make all the rest of your chores easier—not just laundry.

THE MOTHER SHIP

Think of the laundry room like the *brain* of your home. It's the main hub of your organizational journey. This space gives function to so many miscellaneous needs.

We are big fans of having cleaning supplies readily available

for any unforeseen need. Consider this room the mother ship of cleaning. This is the go-to spot. This is the established central zone—a place where you can go every time you need to clean, so you don't end up running around like a mad person looking for one specific cleaning item. Any chance you, too, have multiple glass-cleaner bottles or toilet cleaners scattered around your home? Too often, this decentralization of cleaning supplies leads to multiple products *not* being used. It also means that when there's a mess, the products you need are harder to find. This results in a lot of random sprays and cleaners shoved in odd places—like an upstairs linen closet that rarely gets used. How can you use these supplies if you can't find them when you need them?

This is why we recommend putting everything in one place. This makes it so much easier to maintain. The bonus to this system is that everyone else in the family will know where the cleaning supplies are and—better yet—where to put them back.

When you assess your laundry room right now, maybe you notice you're blessed with ample cabinet space or maybe you're limited to a few shelves. Either way, we can help you make this space work. What we need you to do first is twofold: Take inventory of what you *have*, and then, most important, identify what you actually *use*.

ITEMS THAT STAY IN THE LAUNDRY ROOM

Laundry care supplies

- Laundry detergents
- Stain remover
- Wrinkle release sprays
- Bleach
- Dryer sheets and dryer balls
- Iron
- Clothes steamer
- Lint rollers

Cleaning supplies

- Multipurpose cleaning sprays for the whole house
    - Multi-surface sprays
    - Window cleaner
    - Wood polish
    - Floor cleaner
- Bathroom cleaners (We like keeping most bathroom cleaning items in the laundry room as most of us aren't doing a full cleaning more than once a week.)
- Brooms, mops, floor cleaners
- Magic Erasers and dusters
- Miscellaneous cleaners and sprays (hardware lubricants, leather care, goo removers, silver polish)

Household maintenance items

- Sewing kit
- Light bulbs
- Batteries
- Felt pads
- Nails and adhesive wall hooks
- Tool kits

If you have extra space, here are a few additions to the list.

- **Backup towels.** These are ideal for big messes. If you ever have a leak, random flooding, or the dog comes in from the rain drenched in mud, you know right where to run.
- **Cords.** This is the place to put all those extra charging cords, power strips, and small extension cords for the house.
- **Pest control.** Whether you're using pest sprays or traps, keeping them organized and in one central location can be helpful when you start noticing little bugs inside—and also keeps them out of reach of children or pets.

As you read through this, you're likely realizing how many of these items live in different places all around your home. *Not for long!* As you begin the process of tidying up, gather all the items listed here that are currently scattered throughout your house. We want you to see what you have.

A small caveat: While we love the laundry room being the central place for cleaning supplies, it is perfectly acceptable to keep some cleaning items under the kitchen sink. We recommend having cleaning sprays, sponges, and cleaning gloves there. And as far as bathroom cleaners go, it's up to you and the layout of your home whether you decide to keep them in the laundry room. But we suggest keeping only a toilet bowl cleaner in the bathroom and possibly a daily tile spray if you have hard-to-clean showers. Anything else for your bathroom can be stored in a cleaning caddy in your laundry room for the days you need to clean the house or the bathrooms in particular.

Tidying your cleaning supplies will have ripple effects throughout the entire home.

Tidying your cleaning supplies will have ripple effects throughout the entire home, and once you get this first space under your belt, there's no telling what you can do in the rest of your space.

TIDYING UP

YOUR CLEANING SUPPLIES

LAUNDRY ROOM GOALS

1. Create a clutter-free zone. (This builds motivation.)
2. Identify the key cleaning products you love and use.
3. Optimize the space to function for your laundry and cleaning routine.

PRODUCT LIST

- Wall-mounted broom holder
- Wall-mounted ironing board holder
- Wall-mounted drying rack
- Over-the-door organizer
- Medium-sized turntables for shelves or cabinets
- Lidded bins
- Label maker
- Label tape
- Decor or artwork
- Step stool

Laundry Room Tip #1

FIND WHAT WORKS FOR YOU—AND MAKE IT WORK FOR YOU.

The most important part of tidying up your laundry room is to make the space you have work for how *you* handle laundry and how *you* want to clean your home. Not everyone does laundry the same way or has the same method for cleaning. Some might like to wipe down bathrooms daily, while others tackle cleaning the entire house weekly. Maybe you hire someone to come in and clean for you, and your goal is to make the space as convenient as possible for how that person works best.

If you prefer to stand in the laundry room and fold your laundry directly out of the dryer, a top priority would be to have a countertop cleared off and available. If you have a two-story home, you might prefer keeping a set of cleaning supplies on each level. Think about how you clean your home and the order in which you clean. Reduce any friction you can to make ease and simplicity your priorities. Creating and maintaining a plan to keep this space tidy is useful only when the system works for *your* life and routine.

Laundry Room Tip #2

TAKE INVENTORY AND TOSS.

Laundry rooms can get overrun with excessive laundry and cleaning supplies. Between picking up seasonal scents or impulsively buying a new cleaner that promises to change your life, so many of us have duplicate—or even triplicate—cleaners and tools. When it comes to cleaning supplies, ask yourself, *What do I actually like and really use?*

Pull out all those multiple bottles of the same cleaner that are partially used, barely used, or practically empty. Ask yourself, *Do I like this product? Do I like how it smells? Does this work well?* If not, ask yourself, *Why am I still holding on to it?* We have tried out new laundry detergents only to realize they give us a rash, or we discover our kids' skin is too sensitive, or the fragrance smells too strong. Has that ever happened to you? Do you still keep that bottle of detergent from when your kids were babies? Here's your official permission if you need it: It's okay to give it away or get rid of it! A pretty label might have enticed us to make a purchase, but with cleaning products, sometimes what's tried and true simply works better. If you are holding on to any cleaning products that are nearly empty or that have never been used, ditch the guilt and pitch! Don't worry about any sunk costs, causing you to keep things because you don't want to waste the hard-earned money that you've already invested; the reality is that the money was spent when you bought it, not when you toss it.

Bonus: Creating a consolidated area for supplies means it's easy to see when an item we need is running low and prevents unnecessary purchases.

Laundry Room Tip #3

USE VERTICAL SPACE.

In most homes, laundry rooms tend to be on the smaller side. In many houses, the laundry "room" is more of an area, sometimes just a section of a storage room, garage, or basement. Regardless, it's often a small space that does a *big* job. It holds washing machines, dryers, dirty and clean clothes, cleaning supplies, mops, vacuums, light bulbs, home-repair tools, back-stock supplies, gift wrap, and so on. Utilizing wall space is a great way to tidy up your laundry area. Use as much vertical surface area as you can!

When you use walls, not only will it help you see things at eye level, but it also clears up space from the floor. We like to add a broom holder to hang and organize mops, brooms, and dustpans. Hang your cordless vacuum on the wall, too, so you can quickly charge it after each use. You can also bring in special racks to hang your ironing board and to air-dry your clothing. Another great spot to add some much-needed storage is the back of the door. Use an over-the-door organizer for cleaning bottles, dust cloths, and floor pads.

Laundry Room Tip #4

USE TURNTABLES.

After you've gone through your cleaning products and ditched both the empties and barely used, it's time to make your favorites easier to access. How? Line your cabinet or shelf with turntables! We love designating one turntable per chore: one for laundry care, one for bathroom cleaning, one for dusting, floor care, and so on—depending on your space. A turntable ensures no products get crammed and lost in the back. Just spin that baby around to find what you're looking for. Be sure to label each turntable, too, so everything makes it back to its happy home!

Laundry Room Tip #5

STORE THE ITEMS YOU NEED FOR WASHING CLOTHES BY THE WASHER AND FOR DRYING CLOTHES BY THE DRYER.

That seems like a no-brainer, right? But we are surprised by how often detergent lives across the room from the washer. Since doing laundry is a challenge for many of us, the goal is to make this process as easy and quick as possible. Functionality is key. There's no reason to walk across the room to get the laundry detergent, bleach, fabric softener, dryer sheets, or wool balls every time you start a load. That's a lot of extra steps and inefficiency! Place everything you would use to wash the clothes near or above the washing machine. Remember our tip about vertical space? Apply that here! Place the dryer sheets and wool balls on a shelf right above the dryer. It's a way to make a necessary job just a little bit easier.

Laundry Room Tip #6

VACUUM ATTACHMENTS LIVE TOGETHER.

We all have them—those extra attachments and accessories for the vacuum cleaner. They often end up in every room of the house—a few in the kitchen drawers, one in the mudroom, a couple in the garage. The problem is, without keeping them in one area, you can never find the attachment you need when you need it. If you have a newer cordless vacuum, they typically come with a whole multitude of attachments that are useful for all the tricky spots in your home. We love them; we just want you to *use* them and not lose them.

We suggest storing all these attachments, plus the filters, in a bin together. Add a label and store it on a lower shelf in your laundry room so that it's easy for everyone in the family to grab and help out.

Laundry Room Tip #7

KEEP LIKE WITH LIKE.

This is the golden rule of organization. When categorizing the items in your laundry room, think "like with like." So tape with tape, indoor light bulbs with indoor light bulbs, extension cords with other electrical cords. The next step is to place each category into its own bin and then label it. Once you have all your bins sorted and labeled, it's time to place them on the shelves. And this is where the golden rule of organization comes into play.

Laundry Room Tip #8

WHAT'S NOT USED A LOT GOES UP TOP.

This is another rule of home organization because it just makes sense. This principle, which applies to your entire home, is especially useful for the laundry room.

Store anything that's used only once or twice a year at the very top of your laundry room cabinets or shelves. We're thinking of light bulbs, lanterns, and back-stock cleaning supplies, or holiday decor if you don't have a separate storage area. Store any items that are used monthly on the middle shelves. This might include things like tape, glue, tools, and extension cords. The lowest spot on the shelves, the most easily accessible, is saved for items that are used weekly or daily, such as frequently used cleaning products, laundry care, and batteries. A step stool is *key* to this system, since you want to be able to easily access the top shelving.

Laundry Room Tip #9

AESTHETICS MATTER, EVEN HERE.

It might seem a little silly to decorate a space that's so utilitarian. But in our experience, we've found that when clients bring in pretty decor or artwork to the laundry room, it makes the area feel more inviting and enjoyable. Not only does this help increase motivation to spend time there, but an aesthetically pleasing space can also help you feel less stressed and more connected to the rest of your home and family—even if you are sequestered away folding laundry.

What might you add to your laundry room to make it feel cozier? We like to suggest adding some art to the walls, a pretty rug to the floor, and if you have windows, a few plants to bring some life into the space. Feeling extra? Place a cute lamp on the countertop and a pretty woven basket for all those dirty clothes!

LEVEL UP WHERE YOU CLEAN

Cabinets, baby! One of our favorite ways to level up a laundry room is to take out the old wire shelving and replace it with cabinets. This change allows you to take advantage of the height of your space and maximizes those unused inches available on your walls. There are many cost-effective ways to add cabinetry, such as the in-stock options immediately available at various hardware and home-improvement stores. Cabinets not only elevate the look of the room; they can also add a surprising amount of storage space. We've added cabinets in numerous laundry rooms, and every client has been thrilled with having one cohesive space for all their cleaning and laundry needs.

SQUARE FOOTAGE PROBLEMS?

If this is a concern, the principles still apply. We realize that many people don't have laundry rooms at all. Perhaps you have a stackable unit in a closet or a washer and dryer in the corner of a multipurpose storage area. You may have read this chapter and quickly realized your laundry area won't accommodate everything we've mentioned. Instead, what it can hold is *only* what's necessary for doing laundry—nothing more. If this sounds like you, the general principles still apply: Take inventory and toss, keep like with like, and place rarely used items up high. Cleaning supplies should be streamlined enough after going through this process that they will take up only a small space in a closet or on the back of a door.

MANTRA

Ditch *and* pitch.

Chapter Two

TIDYING UP YOUR PANTRY

There's no getting around it: Cleaning out the pantry can be a beast of a task. But we are ready to dive right into it with you. Whether you have a full walk-in pantry or use just a few upper cabinets in your kitchen, figuring out where and how to store all the food items you need can feel taxing. And depending on how many people you have in your home, coming up with a system that works for everyone is key to maintaining this space *and* keeping it functional.

It's not about having *more* space; it's about using the space you have well.

For most of my adult life, I used one or two upper cabinets in my kitchen and designated them as pantry space. I came up with a system that was functional and sustainable. And now, at the age of thirty-five, I have my first decent pantry. It's a simple reach-in, and we make it work for seven people. This is why we're confident that you can make your space—*any* space—work for you and those you live with. Again, it's not about having *more* space; it's about using the space you have well.

OWNING YOUR REALITY

The biggest challenge with organizing food is identifying what kind of lifestyle you actually have. Of course, most of us want to be people who cook every meal at home, fresh from our gardens and sourced from animals nourished on open green pastures. It's a lovely idea. But many of us buy bagged salads and cheese crisps and get on with our day. No judgment here!

Between the two of us, we have six kids in our homes, and our biggest priority is making sure they are fed—and then fed at least twenty more times again each day. (Kidding aside, they do eat more than you'd imagine.) Because of this, in our pantries, you'll find our favorite packaged snacks, breakfast items, dinner ingredients, what feels like one thousand kid snacks, and our go-to baking items. We cook 80 percent of our meals at home and eat out for about 20 percent. This is the balance that works for us.

But this is just *our* lifestyle. You could be a full-time working mom of a busy family. Or maybe you work part-time from home and spend the afternoons in a minivan doing school drop-offs and pickups, and then running to and from practices through dinner. Maybe you're able to prepare some food items at home but end up needing to grab subs on the way to a baseball game and fast food on the way home. Then there's the single gal reading this who is living her best life in her downtown apartment with the smallest amount of food storage we've ever seen. Naturally, her pantry needs are far different from a mom of three. Your pantry will always look different from the next person's, but what's important is that it works for you.

We have organized for several people who don't need a lot of room for packaged food or dry ingredients because they are primarily a fresh-food family. Then there are others who have a lot of packaged foods. It's necessary to think about your *actual* lifestyle, not your ideal version, before tackling the pantry. Lifestyle is the starting point and gives us a road map so we can know what foods to store and how to store them.

IDENTIFY YOUR WHY

Imagine opening the door of your pantry and right away seeing the box of macaroni and cheese you want to cook for your kids instead of having to dig around or move ten other boxes to find it. It's not a dream; it's possible! Creating a system that easily gets the food from your pantry or fridge to your dining table is the top priority for tidying up the spaces that hold your food.

But the benefits of having an organized pantry are so much more than just creating a space that's calming and easy to look at throughout the day. It even goes beyond saving you time. While these aspects are beneficial by themselves, a workable system will also save you money! If you can see everything you have, that means no more buying extra spaghetti noodles because you didn't remember whether you had any. We once had a client who had at least fifteen boxes of coarse salt—all because they couldn't see what was already there. No one needs that many boxes of salt! The goal here is to quickly see what you have in your pantry, fridge, or freezer and also see what you're running low on.

Knowing why you're organizing this space and what you want from it will help motivate you to create a system and maintain it.

KNOW YOUR LIFESTYLE

Ask yourself these three important lifestyle questions.

- Do more than two people live in the home?
- Do you cook on a regular basis throughout the week?
- Does your household grab packaged food for snacks or meals throughout the week?

If you answered yes to any of these questions, you will need more pantry room for storing and accommodating food.

When you are gearing up to organize a food storage space, think about the meals you make most often. Are you a breakfast guy or girlie? Do you make your lunch for work or plan to eat out? Do you love family dinners around your table?

Restocking items you already have is the most common problem with pantry storage.

Personally, I'm a breakfast and lunch type of woman. I really could live without eating dinner. And when I say *lunch*, what I really mean is "all the snacks I've thrown into my lunch box." My pantry is full of several breakfast items and tons of packaged snacks. Because I'm always on the go, this works for my lifestyle. By the time I get home from a long day at work, I'm spent. (Honestly, give me some cheese and grapes and I'm good!) What you eat most and make often will determine what and how much you'll need to store.

When food is kept in an unorganized, hodgepodge, topsy-turvy way, we lose track of what we have. Even if you know you bought more mac 'n' cheese boxes a few days ago, how often do you stare into that pantry space wasting time or simply go back to the grocery store and load up on more, all because you can't find what you thought you had? Restocking items you already have is the most common problem with pantry storage.

MAKE IT WORK FOR EVERYONE

If you have kids, another consideration for this space is how self-sufficient you want your kids to be. Every household is so different when it comes to this concept, so we want to reiterate that there is no pressure or judgment for how this works for your family. We've seen it all—from full-service chef mom to total self-serve kids. Our role is to come alongside whatever works best for you.

> **When we don't have to stop what we're doing to get them snacks or monitor what they're eating, this creates what we like to call "brain freedom."**

In our homes, we have kids old enough to grab their own snacks, and we want them to. Do they still ask for snacks and want us to get them for them? Of course! But our pantries are set up for the kiddos to help themselves. When we don't have to stop what we're doing to get them snacks or monitor what they're eating, this creates what we like to call "brain freedom"—when we can keep focusing on what we were already focusing on without interruption. This allows for more time to accomplish the tasks at hand.

If you don't want your kiddos to have constant access to food, your pantry will be set up differently from ours.

Or maybe you share your space with roommates instead of

kids. Still, we suggest sorting the food by designating shelf space for each person. That way no one gets upset with anyone for eating their expensive organic crackers.

So let's break it down. How you lay out a pantry is determined by the following:

- **Lifestyle:** How busy are you? How often do you cook at home?
- **Pantry size:** Do you have a pantry (either reach-in or walk-in) or a cabinet or two (and if so, are they small or large)?
- **Favorite foods and meals:** What types of food do you keep the most of? Do you enjoy packaged products or rely more heavily on fresh produce? Are you a frequent baker?
- **Access:** If you have kids, do you want them to be able to grab their own snacks? If you have roommates, how do you want to keep each person's food separate?

FRIDGE FIASCO

You may have noticed that we haven't touched on refrigerators yet—let alone freezers. Both are places that can store—and accumulate—a lot of food. Real talk? Refrigerators and freezers can be hard to maintain, y'all! Even for us. Not to be dramatic, but refrigerators and freezers are the bane of an organizer's existence. But have no fear: We have practical steps for storing and keeping food, which we'll share with you.

The keys to refrigerator organization are:

- Stocking it as minimally as you can
- Meal prep
- Just not having a fridge (*kidding!*)

Refrigerators can hold a lot and yet not enough at the same time. That's what makes them so tricky. Many condiments require refrigeration after opening, and we often see armies of bottles in fridges. We recommend being as selective as you can when it comes to the condiments you keep. But also remember that *you* get to decide what stays and what goes.

Want to guess how many bottles of hot sauce are in my fridge right now? *More than ten!* Can you sense my annoyance? Many of us live with other people, and if you, like me, have someone who cares a whole lot about hot sauce—or mustards, or vinegars, or whatever—getting minimal in those areas might not go over very well. Work with what you have and in a way that keeps the peace.

Obviously, a refrigerator can hold more than just condiments. There are also fresh veggies and fruits, plus all the milks, cheeses, eggs, and meats to consider. If this were all, a refrigerator would be relatively easy to maintain. But amid all that, there are also the pudding cups, applesauce pouches, any drinks you love, yogurts . . . and that's not even mentioning leftovers.

Though this list is hardly exhaustive, we want to encourage

you to use the basic principles of organization for both the fridge and freezer. Keep what you love and use, create zones, keep "like with like," and revise as necessary. In order to keep these spaces tidy, we suggest going through both the fridge and freezer weekly. *Yes, weekly!* This will ensure you're tossing what's old, moving products that need to be consumed closer to the front, and being aware of what you need to replenish.

Based on your lifestyle, let's create a system for food storage so you have what you want when you want it.

So look at your season of life and who lives with you. What do you want your food spaces to do for you and for those in your home? Based on your lifestyle, let's create a system for food storage so you have what you want when you want it.

TIDYING UP

YOUR PANTRY

PANTRY GOALS

1. Create a streamlined system to get food to the table.
2. Build a road map for your pantry and fridge.
3. Find ways to build independence in kids.

PRODUCT LIST

- Airtight canister set
- Plastic bins in multiple sizes
- Lidded bins
- Baskets in multiple sizes
- Medium turntables
- Large turntables
- Label maker
- Label tape
- Bin clips

Pantry Tip #1

REMOVE ORIGINAL PACKAGING.

The first thing we do when organizing a pantry is to pull out every item from the space. The second is to remove the store packaging from any items that are individually packed, such as breakfast foods like oatmeal pouches and granola bars, as well as snacks like small chip bags and jerky sticks. Why take the time to do this after each grocery run? Well, when you keep the items in their boxes, you can't see when they're running low. Only when you put your hand in and come out with nothing do you realize you're out. No one wants to discover they're out of their favorite cereal by pouring into a bowl and getting only cereal dust. What a horrible way to start the day!

The other benefit to removing the packaging is that kids can easily grab their own snacks, which is a win when they ask for food every two hours.

Pantry Tip #2

DECANT, DECANT, DECANT.

Decant means to gradually pour from one container to another. It's often associated with wine, but we like to use this word to convey a concept that's essential in the world of organizing. If you search for "decanting pantry" online, you'll see photo after photo with endless options for canisters of decanted snacks and cooking ingredients. We recommend decanting for two types of pantry items: First, for the items you use all the time. And second, for baking ingredients because they last longer in airtight containers.

At our house, we decant spaghetti noodles, white rice, the three cereals my family eats, and the four most popular snacks. That's it! As lovely as it looks in pictures, we actually don't want to spend the time decanting every single thing we bring home from the grocery store. And we know we would never really keep up with that type of system. We want a plan we can maintain.

Decanting is great for foods that aren't individually wrapped or for the foods your family goes through on a weekly basis. Again, this helps you easily see what you're running low on. Investing in good quality canisters, especially those with an airtight seal, also makes a huge difference in food shelf life, especially for baking powders and other baking ingredients.

Pantry Tip #3

CREATE A KIDS' SNACK SECTION.

As we've mentioned, our kids ask for *a lot* of snacks! If yours are the same, we want to help you create a system that helps them help *you*. To do this, we like to bring all the kid-friendly snacks down to a shelf near the bottom of the pantry or fridge. In our experience, kids will get to the snacks they want even if they have to scale the pantry like a monkey. The nice thing about creating a kid-friendly section is that you get to choose what goes in it. If your priority is to encourage healthy eating, stock options you feel good about them having. This plan is also a great way for your little ones to develop independence. Allowing them to make their own choices at snack time is exciting, and it just might eliminate disagreements.

Pantry Tip #4

KEEP ITEMS IN PLAIN VIEW SO THEY'RE NEVER IGNORED.

We want our pantries to be organized so our most frequently used items are in reach from waist to eye level. No one should need to get on a step stool every morning to reach up high, nor should they have to crouch down super low to find their favorite foods. Placing items where you can see them guarantees you'll find what you're looking for *and use* what you've already bought. This is so important! Not only will you know what you have from day to day, but again, it's easy to keep track of when you need to buy more of anything.

Pantry Tip #5

STORE BAKING SUPPLIES ON A TOP SHELF.

Despite wanting to have them on hand at all times—just in case we want to make that banana bread—most of us rarely use our baking supplies. The majority of us bake only two to three times a year. If this is you, there is zero reason to store baking items on the coveted middle or bottom shelf of the pantry. Remember, reserve those easy-to-access shelves for items that are used daily or weekly. Baking supplies can be stored on top shelves instead, and you can use bins with lids to hold any baking tools: Think cookie cutters, cupcake liners, and icing bags and tips. Using a bin with a lid means you don't have to worry about items getting dusty or grimy.

Airtight canisters are great for baking powders and other ingredients you don't use very often. These can be placed up top as well. We suggest storing the more frequently used dry ingredients, like sugar and flour, a little lower if you use them more often.

Of course, if you *do* bake every week or even monthly, it makes sense to store your supplies a little lower. In this case, we still advise using airtight containers with lids and keeping the smaller loose items together.

Pantry Tip #6

BINS, BINS, BINS!

When we organize, we think about food in categories, and then we divide them into containers or bins. This will create an easy road map for your pantry and ensures everyone in the family knows where to look for an item and—most important—where to put it back. The "putting back" is the key for maintaining a tidy pantry space. When dividing food into categories, we suggest the following:

- Breakfast
- Lunch
- Dinner
- Snacks
- Chips
- Sweet treats
- Baking
- Canned goods
- Condiments

No more shoving your groceries onto a random shelf and closing the door! Every item will have a happy home in a designated space that's predictable and easy to find. The bonus side of this setup? You can tell your spouse exactly where to look for the marinara sauce while you're cooking dinner. And if they still can't find it . . . well . . . you're not alone.

We often buy our organizing bins and accessories from big-box stores. (We do offer a lot of specifics on our social media posts, if you want to follow along with us there.) But there are so many options on the market, and so many unique needs, we want you to choose what works for your space and budget.

Pantry Tip #7

ADD TURNTABLES TO PANTRY CORNERS.

You can never go wrong with a turntable, and using one in a pantry is no exception. Too often, the corners of a pantry are dead spaces where items end up hiding, never to be seen again. But you can easily fix this problem by placing large turntables in those hard-to-reach corners. Turntables will ensure that each item gets some face time and nothing gets lost in the abyss. We suggest storing canned goods and condiments on them, as most people have a large collection of both in their pantries.

Efficiency Tip

If you're tidying up an already-stocked pantry, check the expiration dates on every can and bottle before placing them on the turntable. You might be shocked by how many are out of date. Since there is no reason to store unusable, out-of-date food, toss them. We recommend deep cleaning your pantry once every six months. This is different than straightening up; deep cleaning means pulling out all items, wiping down shelving, and purging what is expired or stale. If you stay up-to-date on these deep cleans, you'll see they get easier and easier because you'll have fewer and fewer items each time, and you'll have the system down!

Pantry Tip #8

KEEP A CONDIMENT TURNTABLE IN YOUR REFRIGERATOR.

Speaking of turntables (have we mentioned we love them?), don't forget to show your refrigerator some organizing love. To be honest, we're not that big on the viral over-the-top fridge organizing, no matter how nice it looks in a picture. Because it's such an overused spot, and the entire family is in and out of it all through the day, rigid systems rarely last long. That said, we do highly recommend adding a turntable to your refrigerator to store your condiments. Most fridges are overflowing with condiments, many of which are shoved into the door shelves. We love to put a nice, big turntable on one of the fridge shelves. Once again, when everything can be seen, nothing gets lost or forgotten. Remember, you can adjust the shelving in your fridge to accommodate the height of your items!

Pantry Tip #9

ORGANIZE THE REST OF THE FRIDGE (IF YOU'RE VERY BRAVE).

Organizing your perishables based on common principles is the easiest game plan for your refrigerator. Typically, you'll store your veggies and fruits in the crisper drawers, corralling dairy items like yogurt, cottage cheese, and sour cream together—and the same for dips like salsa and hummus. Inevitably, you'll keep your meats and cheeses in a drawer as well. Our biggest tips for the fridge are these: Don't be afraid to bring in more bins to separate the categories, make sure to leave ample space for leftovers, and give your fridge a deep clean quarterly.

Pantry Tip #10

MAINTAIN YOUR FREEZER.

Because there's little pressure to eat what's in the freezer immediately, it tends to be much easier than a fridge to maintain. While a bad smell will alert you to an unused bag of broccoli in the fridge, a bag of frozen broccoli can live in the freezing cold for a pretty long time. We encourage our clients to identify their favorite things to store. In my freezer, it's most important to keep fruit for smoothies, breakfast sandwiches or premade pancakes (especially helpful for the kids during the school year), some veggies, a couple of pizzas, and a small amount of sweet treats, like ice cream. Since there's less stuff to store here, it's easier to organize. For folks who like to stock up on meats, they typically invest in a deep freezer so it doesn't take up all their precious easy-to-access freezer space.

Pantry Tip #11

ADD LABELS TO EACH BIN AND BASKET.

We've given everything a place. We know where it goes—but what about your spouse, your sister, your mother-in-law, your kids, or your kids' friends? They won't walk into the pantry and instinctively know where to tuck the bag of chips they almost finished. This is where labels come into play.

We suggest labeling every bin, basket, and turntable so it's clear for family members and guests alike. Keep the labels general so when you change up a specific item, you don't have to redo the labels. Snacks can just be "snacks." The same goes for breakfast items, cereals, chips, and so on. Labels can be cute or practical, but each one plays an important role in keeping everything tidy where you eat.

Many affordable label makers are on the market these days, and we suggest investing in one. Our favorites connect to your phone through Bluetooth, so you can type right on your phone's keyboard! You can also find clips that hook on to your baskets that you can add labels to as well.

LEVEL UP YOUR PANTRY

Add a storage solution. Even after tidying up, some of us may still feel like we're maxed out on space. Level up by purchasing a storage piece for your kitchen or dining space. We've worked with several clients who needed to divide their pantry items because of space constraints, so we decided to keep snacks and go-to items in one place and dry pantry goods in another. Many online stores have great hutches and storage cabinets that can fit into a variety of spaces, big or small. Adding a separate piece for additional storage will ensure this area stays tidy and is easy to maintain. You can also invest in an over-the-door organizer that gives you a little extra space to store smaller items like spices, drinks, cans, or paper goods.

SQUARE FOOTAGE PROBLEMS?

Divide and conquer. If you're currently storing your food in a single upper cabinet, you're not alone. We've been there and know how tricky it is. Turntables are your best friends, as well as a step stool. Using the entire height of the cabinet is key. We recommend dividing the space by types of meals and snacks. For example, a breakfast shelf, a dinner shelf, condiments and oils on another, and if you have the room, baking at the very top. Keeping the shelves separated like this will help you maintain your space for the long haul.

MANTRA

Bins *for the* win!

Chapter Three

TIDYING UP

WHERE YOU COOK

Whether you're a skilled home chef or you regularly feed your people cereal for dinner, the most-used space in a home is the kitchen. The kitchen is where we find connection and comfort. Across cultures and generations, people instinctively congregate around food in the places that nourish them most. The kitchen is the heart of the home.

The kitchen is the heart of the home.

As lovely as it is to have such a space for preparing meals and offering them to those we love, maintaining a kitchen can be a struggle. Because this space is so central to our lives and to those we love, it can also become a space of chaos—and fast. All the daily activity leads to dishes piled high in the sink, dirty pans on the stove, cluttered countertops, piles of papers, crumbs on the floor, and *Where are the keys?* How you move and feel in the heart of your home matters.

STREAMLINE

Think through those first steps as you begin cooking, pouring oil, and grabbing spices. Think about how you load and unload your dishwasher, or even how you replace your trash bag liner. Busy lives require efficiency—and ease of movement is key.

If you are cooking dinner and your trash can is full, it doesn't make sense to run to the laundry room to grab a new bag. If you're hosting a bunch of kids for a slumber party, it's important to have paper plates and disposables in an easily accessible spot to keep cleanup simple. As children grow and become more self-sufficient, we encourage parents to create a kid-friendly zone that makes it easy for the kids to help themselves. This saves parents time . . . and sanity!

DOES IT HAVE A HOME?

Having a "home"—a singular, designated place—for everything in our kitchens is neither high-maintenance nor asking for too much. And it sets up the whole family for success. Everyone—even guests—will know where to find items and where to put them back. Where you put your knives, towels, carrot peeler—all of it matters. We've discovered from implementing this in our own lives and for our clients that these efforts typically have a calming effect, which in turn can make our days flow better and set our minds at ease. Tidying up our kitchens is just one way we can say goodbye to the dysregulation and chaos, and welcome peace and well-being into a space we frequent every day.

This doesn't mean your kitchen needs to be boring. We encourage balance. Our goal here is to find a middle ground where practicality meets warmth—a place where your friends feel welcome *and* you can find your potato peeler. So to start, we invite you to identify what you like about your kitchen. Think functionally, aesthetically, and emotionally.

Please take a few minutes to think through the following questions:

- What do I like about my kitchen?
- What role or purpose do I want for my kitchen?
- How do I want my kitchen to feel for myself and those I love?

Your answers here are the key to where you start tidying up your kitchen. And they will give you a measurable goal to focus on as well as the why to keep you going.

I love my kitchen counters and that my silverware drawer is so close to the dishwasher. But more than anything, I love that the

Having an intention for your kitchen creates a deeper purpose, one that becomes the true motivation for keeping the space tidy.

kitchen is where my family gathers and where I can cook them good, nourishing food. I like that my kitchen is a place for connection in the morning, before our days get going, and where there's always room for one more person for dinner. I therefore want it to be a place my family can leave from and come home to and feel calm and cared for.

See? Practical *and* emotional. Having an intention for your kitchen creates a deeper purpose, one that becomes the true motivation for keeping the space tidy. When we identify what we want to keep as the steady undercurrent for a space, it makes the work of getting tidy—and maintaining it—much easier.

In our homes, we prioritize a coziness that dances seamlessly with organization. We like cookbooks and viney plants decorating our kitchen because it makes us feel peace and joy while we do the dishes, wipe counters, and chop vegetables. But the drawers and cabinets are functional and practical; everything has a home. Nothing hangs out on the counter, waiting to be put away somewhere. When we cook or bake, whether we need a certain utensil, pot, or appliance, we not only know where it is, but it's easily accessible. Organized. Cozy. Balanced.

THE 80/20 RULE

Some of the most common complaints we hear about kitchens are:

- Not enough drawer space
- Lower cabinets become black holes of chaos
- Lack of flow or feeling of inefficiency
- Confusion about how to best use corner cabinets
- "Catchall" countertops
- Not knowing how or where to store small appliances

Lack of storage space is probably the most frequently identified frustration in the kitchen. A lack of space can be a very real thing, as some homes are simply small or were designed in a different era that had different standards with fewer appliances on the market. And we've also seen homes with kitchens designed by people who must not have had actual humans in mind because of how small and impractical they are. But most people struggle less with the storage space itself and more with owning too much stuff. We want our clients to keep as much as they

Lack of storage space is probably the most frequently identified frustration in the kitchen.

want or need, to find a place to put it all, and to make it all work. But sometimes things do have to go.

So how does a person decide what to keep and what to let go of? We like to adhere to the 80/20 rule. While kitchens can serve a big role for how a family feels, the space itself shouldn't feel like the equivalent of an emotional bubble bath. Nor should it be as sterile and unwelcoming as an operating room. Kitchens should be 80 percent efficiency, 20 percent emotional.

Let's talk about the 20 percent first. Most people have some type of dish or drinkware that has been passed down by family and holds a significant amount of emotional weight. Like Grandma's china, those crystal champagne flutes from your wedding, that vase or platter or pitcher you bought on a trip with your family. Even if you don't use an item regularly, you simply may not be ready or willing to part with it. When this happens, we ask our clients, "How can you keep and honor these pieces, giving you access to this emotional connection, and still have an efficient and functional space?"

Kitchens should be 80 percent efficiency, 20 percent emotional.

We can't tell you how many "Santa's Cookies" plates we've come across during the process of organizing kitchens. Almost all our clients want to keep them—and rightly so. Is there anything sweeter than those years of family memories? Of course you can keep that plate!

But when one item stays, this means something else must go. It's completely your decision, but there will need to be sacrifices somewhere. So yes, we believe you should keep sentimental items; you'll just have to get serious about those ten spatulas in your utensil crock. An emotional keep means adding something else to the donation heap.

Maybe you'd hold on to Mamaw's dishes but purge the pots and unmatched storage containers you never use. Keep the crystal, get rid of the linen napkins. Enjoy the cereal bowl your son painted when he was five, but donate the salad bowl you received as a hostess gift last winter. You don't have to purge everything that holds meaning, but you do have to choose how to revise your space and make it work better *for you.*

This leads us to the 80 percent: functionality and efficiency. We find that after you work through the emotional decisions of what to keep and what to throw away or donate, this part of tidying up your kitchen actually goes surprisingly fast. Why? Because you have objective information when you determine how often you use certain items. Daily? Weekly? Rarely? Seasonally?

We're guessing you're already thinking of a few items you can donate and a few you want to keep. You're also likely taking a mental inventory of what you use every day but keep in a hard-to-reach place or what you don't use that often but store in an easily accessible cupboard or drawer, occupying coveted space. You might also be thinking of your unique kitchen and your specific needs, which is why we want to dive a little deeper into some of the most common areas of concern when we work with clients in their kitchens.

The intentionality behind tidying up your kitchen spaces will give you the biggest payback ever.

We love walking into our kitchens every morning, pouring some coffee, and not having anything fall out of the cabinet. We love being able to find what we need when we need it. We love starting and ending our days with a feeling of calm. We want this for you too.

The intentionality behind tidying up your kitchen spaces will give you the biggest payback ever. We want your kitchen to embody all the coziness of a lit candle on a cold night or a warm fall sweater when the weather turns. This is the feeling we're going for. Big, cozy, practical solutions that make you so happy to call your home yours.

TIDYING UP

WHERE YOU COOK

KITCHEN GOALS

1. Pare down kitchen items that largely go unused.
2. Create a spot for every item that lives in the kitchen.
3. Create a kitchen layout that maximizes efficiency and functionality.

PRODUCT LIST

- Different-sized drawer bins with straight sides
- Silverware organizer
- Shelf risers
- Extra-large turntables
- Medium turntables
- Adhesive storage bins
- Spice drawer liner

Kitchen Tip #1

CREATE ZONES.

Think about how you function in your kitchen from day-to-day. The last thing you want to do while packing school lunches for your kiddos is to walk across the kitchen five times. Create a layout for your cabinets and drawers that promotes peak efficiency as you move around the space. Designate a drawer or cabinet, for example, that holds everything you need for packing lunches: lunch boxes, storage bags, water bottles, and utensils. Apply this zone concept to your entire kitchen.

Doing the dishes? Create a zone under your sink for everything you need to complete the task without having to walk away to grab a sponge from your pantry. The key is to make your kitchen zones functional for every task you handle on a daily basis. This will allow you to tackle things easily and get on with enjoying your day.

Kitchen Tip #2

MEASURE FIRST, BUY SECOND.

As professional organizers, part of our job is to bring in products that work for our clients' homes and spaces. Over the years, we've seen our fair share of organizing products that were purchased by our clients who had great intentions but never put them to use. Most often, we discovered it's because they didn't fit in the intended space. That's a lot of wasted time and money. Please, measure your drawer spaces or cabinets before purchasing any organizing products.

Also, you'll want any organization tool to help you utilize the *entire* space. For drawers, avoid bins with tapered sides. You want to get the most out of every square inch.

Kitchen Tip #3

USE THE LEVEL METHOD.

We use this method to tackle where items will live in the kitchen. Keep daily used items between eye and waist level. Weekly used items can be tucked into a lower cabinet. And seasonal or rarely used items can easily go up high—truly perfect for that weird cabinet above the oven or refrigerator!

Kitchen Tip #4

MAKE THE MOST OF YOUR DRAWER SPACE.

When we think about the layout of the kitchen, we love having some key drawer essentials. Our must-haves for drawers include a dish towel drawer that's preferably placed close to the sink for easy access. Even if you don't feel like you have enough drawers, we really believe every home needs a junk drawer. Third, please have a silverware drawer, for obvious reasons! Last, we love keeping a drawer for cooking or food prep utensils; this ultimately keeps the counters pretty clear.

If you have more drawers than this, great! Start here and keep going. Our suggestions beyond the list above would be a baking utensil drawer, a drawer for storage bags and food wrap (cling wrap and aluminum foil), and a drawer for storage containers. Part of the tidying-up process is taking ownership and feeling empowered to use the drawers in a way that works best for you.

Kitchen Tip #5

STORE SILVERWARE BY THE DISHWASHER.

This is one of the first changes we make when organizing a client's kitchen. More often than not, the utensils are in a drawer across the kitchen, making unloading the dishwasher an incredibly tedious job. But if you can pull the pieces out of the caddy and place them straight into a drawer without taking a step, that saves you time and makes the task feel a tad bit easier.

Efficiency Tip

Load the silverware into the dishwasher caddy by categories: forks together, spoons together, and knives together. This way, you can reach into the caddy and grab forks and place them into their spot in your silverware organizer in one motion. No extra time spent sorting as you unload!

Kitchen Tip #6

RECONSIDER YOUR DRINKWARE COLLECTION.

Go through all your drinkware and divide it into two groups: keep and donate. Most people have an overstuffed cabinet full of cups and glasses that they can hardly see, let alone use. So think through how you live and how many you really need. Do you host weekly family meals? Do you often have overnight guests? Do you throw dinner parties? Keep only what will actually be used for your family's lifestyle. If you always use disposable cups when you have a party, you probably don't need to keep extra glassware. Keep only what makes practical sense. (If you do host fancy dinner parties, keep the barware but consider streamlining your coffee mugs!) Donate excess mugs, plastic cups, and barware. Again, it's a give-and-take situation. There's no one correct number for everyone.

Efficiency Tip

Store coffee mugs in a cabinet above your coffee maker. We also love to use shelf risers to double the number of mugs you can store on one shelf!

Kitchen Tip #7

MOVE THOSE SHELVES!

Have you ever noticed the little peg holes on the internal walls of your kitchen cabinets? Those holes are for moving the shelves higher or lower. Most cabinets have two to three shelves, and the majority of people never adjust them—*but you should!* It's an easy way to customize your kitchen and make the shelves work for your items and your height.

If you have tall wine glasses that you regularly use but they won't fit on the middle shelf, don't give up and tuck them away in a hard-to-reach cabinet (like that upper corner cabinet top shelf). Instead, move the top shelf up, and make space for them where you can reach them. If you are on the shorter side height-wise, you shouldn't have to grab the step stool whenever you want something from the second shelf or above. Just move the second shelf down. Remember: Always use the lowest shelves of your upper kitchen cabinets for daily-use items and save those top shelves for less frequently used items.

Kitchen Tip #8

BIG SPACE EQUALS BIG ITEMS.

Lower cabinets are often very deep. Usually, they're double the depth of upper cabinets. They're so deep, you might have to get on your hands and knees to reach for whatever has been shoved toward the back. Lower cabinets are ideal spots for becoming black holes. One time, we found a whole Barbie family living in a lower cabinet! Evicted from the kitchen, we moved them back to their home with the other toys.

When organizing lower cabinets, follow the principle of ensuring the space fits the item. Big space equals big items. If you place a bunch of smaller items into a large space, they're much more likely to get lost and disorganized. The big items we suggest living in lower cabinets include larger appliances or gadgets you aren't using every day, such as slow cookers, food processors, Instant Pots, air fryers, mixers, blenders, and so on. The more frequently used items should be most accessible. Having a cabinet (or two) for pots and pans is a must. Just be careful with those lids; they're small and can become chaotic quickly. Luckily, there are lots of lid-storage options on the market.

Kitchen Tip #9

ADD LARGE TURNTABLES TO DEEP CORNER CABINETS.

You can't beat the storage space that corner cabinets offer. Unfortunately, they are usually so deep that unless you're willing to tweak your neck while contorting your body, too many items get lost in the back, rarely to be seen again. When you can't see what you have or forget what has been stored back there, all that extra space becomes pointless.

To remedy this, we like to use large turntables. These handy tools allow you to store items without any getting crowded or lost in the very back. As you spin that baby around, every item is on display. Turntables are a must-have for cooking oils, protein powders, baking ingredients, supplements, medications, and more.

Kitchen Tip #10

USE THE DOOR SPACE, INCLUDING THE BACKS OF YOUR CABINET DOORS.

This is one of our favorite organizing secrets. Since almost everyone wishes they could add a little more square footage and storage space to their home, we see the backs of doors as usable space—from closet doors to bedroom doors to bathroom doors and, yes, even cabinet doors.

We also like to use small adhesive bins and attach them to the inside of kitchen cabinets. These are small enough to fit in tight spaces and come with adhesive pads so you can literally stick them to any spot. Need an easy grab-and-go place to store your dishwasher pods? Add an adhesive bin to the back of your under-sink cabinet. Not sure where to store your reusable straws? Add an adhesive bin to the back of the cabinet door where you keep your to-go cups. Just think of all the added storage!

Kitchen Tip #11

STORE SPICES IN A DRAWER.

We've seen every possible way to store spices: tiered risers, narrow pull-out cabinets, back-of-the-door racks. But we stand, and will always stand, by using a drawer for your spices. We suggest using a drawer next to your cooktop so you can easily grab whatever you need without ever having to move away from your spot in front of the stove.

We use spice drawer liners—yes, there *is* such a thing! A spice drawer liner is a nonslip liner that comes in a roll, and you cut it to fit your drawer. Place your spices down, and no matter how often you open the drawer, they stay in place without sliding or spilling. Bonus points if you use matching spice bottles and line them up in alphabetical order!

Kitchen Tip #12

LARGE PLATTERS AND ENTERTAINMENT PIECES GO ABOVE THE REFRIGERATOR.

We all have those pieces in our kitchen that we rarely use, but it wouldn't make sense to repurchase every time we need them. The problem is, they're just so big. We're thinking about those large platters you use around the holidays to serve meats and sides, cake stands you pull out for showers and birthdays, roasting pans, and extra-large cutting boards for charcuterie displays. When you need them, you *need* them, but this typically occurs only once or twice a year.

These large and rarely used items should not be stored in an everyday spot in your kitchen. Given that you don't need to access them often, we like to store these items in the cabinet above the fridge. It's an underused cabinet in most houses—some people even forget they have it. We know it's not convenient to climb up on a step stool, but that's exactly why it's the perfect spot for these entertainment pieces! You know exactly where they are, but they're not taking up valuable space that would be better for more frequently used items.

Kitchen Tip #13

KEEP THE COUNTERS CLEAR.

Most people we meet have the same desire: a clutter-free kitchen counter. When we see a messy counter, our brains immediately go into overdrive, thinking, *I should clear this off.* But without a designated spot for everything, the task gets pushed aside—and the stress builds. We want you to know this: Your counters *can* be clear, calm, and beautiful. Yes, it's possible. In fact, we believe many people need to hear that reassurance. But keeping counters clear isn't an overnight transformation; it's a learned skill. In many homes today, it's common to have appliances like air fryers, small ovens, or coffee makers on the counter, along with canisters or other everyday items. Some people prefer to keep things like butter, salt, and pepper visible. Since you're about to have an organized junk drawer for things like keys, coins, and stray mail, you can easily tuck away the little things that often clutter your counters.

LEVEL UP WHERE YOU COOK

Install lower cabinet pull-out drawers. One of our favorite ways to level up the kitchen is to add pull-out drawers or glide-out shelves in your lower cabinets. This is an amazing way to access everything in the bottom half of your kitchen without losing anything to the deep darkness of those lower cabinets. Simply measure the width, depth, and height of your cabinet and then order the closest size to fit the space from a home supply store or an online retailer. If you're adding drawers to all the lower cabinets, measure each one. Most cabinet sizes vary, even by a quarter of an inch.

SQUARE FOOTAGE PROBLEMS?

Go vertical. We know many of our readers live in small spaces. Maybe you have an apartment or a tiny home, and you *really* need to maximize the minimal space you have. Our favorite way to stay tidy where you cook is to make sure you always use the height of your space. Yes, the step stool may have to become your new best friend. We encourage our clients with small kitchens to use the very top shelf of your cabinets even for everyday items. If you have deep drawers in your kitchen, use the height of that space too! There are stackable drawer inserts that allow you to layer all your silverware, knives, and go-to kitchen gadgets into your drawer space. You can also find magnetic bins to place on your fridge wall or door for kitchen utensils or spices, ensuring they don't take up precious and limited countertop space.

MANTRA

For the kitchen,
it's 80 percent efficiency,
20 percent emotion.

Chapter Four

TIDYING UP

WHERE YOU GATHER

My first "grown-up" home was a tiny little apartment. We had hand-me-down couches, old bookshelves, a TV, and lots of art. I wanted the space to feel open but cozy—a place for all our friends to come over, hang out, and just *be*. I wanted to create a space centered around love and comfort.

The kitchen is usually where everyone gathers at parties, but from my experience, the living room is where connections grow into relationships. I can't tell you how many bucketloads of tears have been shed with my girlfriends on a living room couch. Or the countless belly laughs, where I have to roll myself over so I don't accidentally pee my pants! Now that I have a larger family, sitting on the couch and watching shows together is one of my all-time favorite things, an activity where we all bond after a long week.

> **Whether you are in your twenties and hosting your very best friends or you have a large family that loves a weekend movie night, gathering spaces deserve a particular kind of attention.**

Whether you are in your twenties and hosting your very best friends or you have a large family that loves a weekend movie night, gathering spaces deserve a particular kind of attention. We want to put this room together with intentionality, to cultivate a sense of peace and safety for all the people in your life. How you organize your living room can directly affect the way you interact with your family and friends. The choice is yours!

TOY FRENZY

If organized poorly, living rooms can unintentionally wind people up. If our stuff is *everywhere,* our nervous systems can become overstimulated—leading to disruptive emotions, irritability, tension, and confusion.[1] When this happens chronically, it can lead to feelings of anxiety and unease. And those are the *last* things we want to feel in our own homes.

I've been there. When my son was a baby, and even well into his toddler years, I felt so overwhelmed by everything we kept in the living space: a baby swing, a jumper, and a walker when he was old enough to move around. All these things were supposed to make our lives easier, but they made the room feel so chaotic. As he grew, those items were replaced with toys—*so many toys*! I clearly remember how often I'd walk through our front door, which opened directly into the living room, and immediately feel an overwhelming wave of anxiety, just from seeing all the *stuff*.

Part of me feels embarrassed to express that, but I want to share this because I know I'm not alone. At that time, when we had little kids, neither of us realized how many others also suffered from anxiety triggered by the clutter in their homes. But now, after working with so many different parents and caretakers, we know how often this happens. We all want to feel centered and peaceful when we walk into our homes. For me, it was a shift in mindset that made the biggest difference. I stopped striving for perfection and embraced the reality that when you have little kids, things are bound to be a little chaotic—and that's *okay*! I realized that as kids grow older, the giant toys disappear and the clutter becomes less overwhelming than it was in the toddler years. What I'm really trying to say is, this phase is just that: a phase. It's temporary, and eventually, the mountain of toys will shrink.

The next step after changing your mindset is creating systems for the things you *can* manage. You might not be able to hide away that giant baby jumper right now, but having baskets or bins for the smaller toys and clutter can make a huge difference. It's all about creating some breathing room so when the overwhelm starts to set in, you can look around and see less. A little order can go a long way in helping you feel more at peace.

We're passionate about organization, but the real purpose of this space is about gathering.

I remember feeling like that season of life would never end, but what they say is true: It really does go fast. Those years have long passed, but I'd like to extend extra grace to those in the throes of young parenthood. Even with the solutions we've created, the toys may stay out longer than you'd like, and your living room may not be picture-perfect all the time, but remember that your kids are having fun and you are fulfilling the purpose of this room: connection.

And that priority of connection goes for those of you who aren't parents too. We're passionate about organization, but the real purpose of this space is about gathering. If you're doing that—connecting with those you love—that's what life is really about.

With that said, let's create the most manageable and inviting living space possible so your relationships can flourish and grow in a peaceful, personalized space. We've got you!

CREATING AN INVITING SPACE

If you haven't noticed by now, evaluating how you want to use your space and identifying what your goals are is the first step for almost every area we discuss. This is so important because everyone uses their spaces differently. This seems basic, but think about it: We all have living rooms, but what we have in the rest of the home will determine how we use this area. For example, if you have a tiny laundry room or use a common laundry space, you might need to fold your clothes in your living room. If you, like us, don't have a playroom, toys will inevitably end up here, and you'll need a solution for keeping them tidy. Some people have additional recreation or bonus rooms that can be used for watching TV and movies or playing video games, so they don't need to worry about storing media in their living rooms.

Think through all the ways you and your family use this area. With this list in hand, you can intentionally set up the space to reflect those priorities. Make getting cozy on the couch super easy. The room *can* function well both for family and friends to gather and for little ones to play.

TIDYING UP

WHERE YOU GATHER

LIVING ROOM GOALS

1. Create a living space that enhances inner peace.
2. Set up systems for quick cleanup.
3. Revise collections.

PRODUCT LIST

- Woven baskets in various sizes
- Plastic bins
- Disc storage box
- Plastic disc sleeves
- Zippered pouches in various sizes
- Large plastic storage totes
- Label maker
- Label tape

Living Room Tip #1

PURGE EXCESS FURNITURE.

Too much furniture is often the main culprit behind a chaotic, overcrowded space. Many of us buy pieces without considering how they'll fit into the flow of the room, then end up cramming them in alongside hand-me-downs from family or friends. Take a moment to look around your space. Do you feel cramped or closed in? A simple way to assess if you have too much furniture is to check if there's a large piece against every wall. If each wall is lined with bulky furniture at roughly the same height, it can make the room feel heavy and congested. The key is to create variety in the dimensions of the room so your eyes aren't overwhelmed by constant visual clutter. A little breathing room goes a long way!

If there's a family item you don't want to part with, *that's okay!* But just like the emotional selections made in the kitchen, you'll similarly need to make creative solutions or revisions elsewhere. For example, if you were given some antique side tables but don't need them in your living room, they might be a better fit for your guest room. Could that passed-down love seat go in a teen's room or in an office? There are so many fun and unique ways to use items you're not ready to part with. The living room should not be the default storage space for extra furniture. The living room should be a space where it's quick to tidy, quick to relax, and quick to gather with those you love.

Living Room Tip #2

DON'T SWEAT THE SMALL STUFF.

Who doesn't love a tchotchke? Many of us fill our living room shelves with knickknacks, souvenirs, photos, and books, often without thinking about how they're styled. Over time, these items can become cluttered and forgotten, making it harder to appreciate the things that truly matter, like a grandparent's wedding photo or your child's artwork. As you declutter, take the opportunity to rediscover these sentimental pieces by intentionally styling your shelves. If you display collections—such as family photos, awards, or DVDs—consider whether they still bring you joy. Sometimes less is more. Reducing the number of photo frames or displayed items can lighten your space and free up mental energy. The key is creating a sense of flow and intentionality so your living room becomes a place you love where the items that truly matter shine, and the rest can be boxed or donated. A little intentional curation can transform your space and make it feel refreshed and alive.

Living Room Tip #3

CREATE A REMOTE CENTRAL.

What's one of the most annoying things in the world? Have you ever gotten tucked in on the couch with your favorite blanket and a bowl of popcorn, ready to binge the latest show, and then you can't find the remote? Every family member is interrogated: *Who had it last?* Fingers are pointed, blame circles around, until someone finds it deep in the side of a couch cushion.

To avoid this, designate one spot for remotes. This may seem like too simple of an idea here, but this one small change will create a huge sense of order and save you so much time. We suggest corralling them all in a small basket or box that lives on a side table. It's important to work on developing the habit of *always* putting the remotes back in their place after each use. This can be a little tricky for children, but over time they will get it!

Living Room Tip #4

FIND PRETTY BASKETS FOR TOYS.

In the absence of a playroom, you'll have to get creative for toy storage in the living room. Kids usually insist on playing in the spaces closest to their parents, and the living room often becomes the default. It's necessary to set up a system for toys here because if you don't, you'll be stepping on toys every time you walk across the room. *Ouch!* LEGO blocks and Barbie shoes are the worst!

A simple system is to bring in one basket for each kiddo in your home. We suggest choosing baskets that match the decor of your living room. As your children bring out toys from their bedrooms to play with in the living room, the mess can escalate quickly. It's unrealistic to expect children to return every little toy to their rooms as soon as they are finished playing with it, especially if they are very young. But even the smallest kids can help clean up at the end of the day with this easy basket system!

Depending on their ages, when the basket is full, either you or they can take it to their rooms and put everything away. This system is especially useful when you are expecting company and the living room is littered with toys. Just toss everything into the baskets and voilà—the living room is presentable!

Living Room Tip #5

USE BINS FOR GAMING ACCESSORIES.

It's difficult to keep up with all the gaming consoles available on the market, let alone the different controllers, headsets, charging stations, and accessories. If you have a gamer in your home, you know how easily this stuff can take over. One minute you're ready to cuddle up on the couch; the next you're sitting on an uncomfortable controller and have no clue what it goes to.

An easy way to keep all these items organized is with individual bins stored by category. Place all the controllers, charging cords, SD cards, and accessories for one gaming device into one bin, then label it. Store the bins close to the television, ideally in a media console or built-in cabinet. When your child (or partner) is looking for a certain controller, instead of turning the whole house upside down, you can simply point to the correct bin. Now *that* sounds like a time and energy saver!

Living Room Tip #6

FIND EFFECTIVE BLU-RAY AND DVD STORAGE.

We are here to tell you something you may not believe: A lot of people still own Blu-rays and DVDs! And some own a *lot* of them. (Shout-out to the VHS collectors out there!) For most, these tend to be more sentimental collections rather than something still in use. Sometimes when people spend hard-earned dollars on certain items, the sunk costs coupled with the memories can make certain items hard to part with. And that's okay.

All that said, we *do* suggest paring down your collection as much as possible because these items take up valuable space in your living room. Keep only the movies that are special to you. If the discs are truly a memento and you wish to keep them in their original boxes, store them in large plastic bins with lids. Keep these bins where you keep other memento items (see chapter 10) and not in the main living space. But if you still use the discs to watch the movies and aren't opposed to tossing the boxes, we suggest storing them like CDs in a sleeved binder or folder. Just take the DVD out of its original packaging and place it into a thin, plastic sleeve. Close to two hundred sleeved discs can be contained within one small storage solution. That's an entire media console's worth of storage revised down to one small box. This is also great if your kids watch DVDs in the car. Before getting on the road, they can quickly grab the whole collection and go.

Living Room Tip #7

KEEP A BASKET FOR BLANKETS CLOSE TO THE COUCH.

There's nothing better in this world than curling up on your couch with a soft, cozy blanket. Can you sense a trend with what we like to do? Some of us (cough, raises hand) are just blanket people. No matter the temp outside, if we're sitting on a couch, we *need* a blanket on our lap. Because of this, we like to always keep a number of blankets within arm's reach in our living rooms. (Not to mention how often blankets are required to build forts in our homes!) Just like with toys, we love to bring in a beautiful basket to hold all the blankets. Generally speaking, baskets add warmth and texture into any space, so it's a great way to keep several blankets handy while elevating the look of a room. A good rule of thumb is to keep one blanket for each person within easy reach. This way, no one has to argue over who gets one. We also recommend swapping blankets seasonally: lighter, breathable options for warmer months, and cozier, heavier blankets when the weather turns cool. This ensures everyone stays comfortable year-round.

Living Room Tip #8

SET UP A SMALL BASKET FOR PET TOYS.

We never want to leave out the furry family members from our tidying-up efforts. Both of us have pets, and we love them like crazy. But the toys that end up all over the house? Not so much. Stepping on a squeaking pet toy in the middle of the night or turning your ankle from its weird shape can practically give you a panic attack. We treat pet toys just like our children's toys—by corralling them in a basket. The only difference with pet toys is that you should choose a low-profile basket so it's easy for them to grab the toy they want to play with. Because most of our furry children don't help us clean up, it's also an easy place to toss them at the end of the day. (Actually, that does sound the same as human children!) Our goal is to have *one* spot for the toys. It won't take long for your pet to know exactly where to go to fetch their favorite plaything.

Living Room Tip #9

RECONSIDER YOUR BOOK COLLECTION.

We can hear so many of you groan at just the thought of downsizing your books. Yes, a beautifully curated bookshelf with color-coordinated spines and sentimental trinkets and artwork sprinkled in can be a great addition to a room. But similar to DVDs, we suggest keeping only those books that you are currently reading, the ones you read over and over, or the ones with sentimental significance to you.

Let us be clear: We *love* books. We read or listen to them every day. We've even written this one! But books can quickly become unruly piles all over your home. (You know who you are!) We really want to help you avoid having your home look like all it's doing is being an overstuffed storage area for all your books. Instead, you can have a meaningful collection that lives beautifully on a bookshelf, one that makes you happy every time you lay eyes on it. For those books you haven't touched in years or that mean nothing to you emotionally, donate them or pass them on to a friend.

Living Room Tip #10

USE ZIPPERED POUCHES FOR STORING BOARD GAMES.

If you love a good game night with family and friends, chances are you own a lot of board and card games. We love this; it's so fun! The downside is that those game boxes take up a lot of space. Have you seen some of these sophisticated boardgames recently? They are huge and can be tricky to store.

If you aren't attached to the game's box, empty out all the contents of your board game into a narrow, zipped pouch. Don't forget anything, of course, or the game will definitely not be as fun! Grab the dice, the cards, the board, the game pieces, and most important, the instructions. Do this for all your board and card games. By tossing the boxes, you will gain at least half of the previously used space back. Be sure to label the outside of the pouch with the name of the game so you can quickly grab it when you want to play. Store the pouches together in a basket near your TV console, on a built-in, or in a nearby closet.

LEVEL UP WHERE YOU GATHER

Cozy it up. Leveling up where you gather is simple: *Make it cozier!* Think about how you can bring in personality and warmth. Once things are organized and in their rightful place, you're going to want to hang out here more. A lot of living rooms we see, even well-organized ones, remain fairly functional. Frame family photos and hang up artwork you like. Select curtains that make the space feel more inviting, such as ceiling-to-floor curtains (which make the room look bigger) in velvet or linen to add texture to the space. We prefer to avoid patterns to reduce the chaos and recommend choosing a neutral or light color. Another great idea is to buy an area rug that ties the entire room together.

We know these aren't organizing tips, but when it comes to the living room, design is very important. It's okay to want your home to feel better and more beautiful. All this, along with tidying up, will help make your gathering space a place where people truly want to spend their time.

SQUARE FOOTAGE PROBLEMS?

Make your furniture do double duty. If you have a small living room, every piece of furniture needs to be functional *and* have storage. So many living room pieces out there are minimalist and lovely, but if they lack storage features, it's not practical for a small space. So invest in pieces that allow you to tuck away the clutter. We suggest end tables with drawers. A coffee table or ottoman with storage space. TV consoles with cabinets. When you can store blankets, books, remotes, and games away and out-of-sight, your space will feel bigger and be so much easier to keep tidy.

MANTRA

The place you gather is a space that matters.

Chapter Five

TIDYING UP

WHERE YOU GET READY

Have you ever had a day start off on the wrong foot because the morning was so hectic and wild? You're frantically looking for your earrings, and then one of your kids shouts for you to help them find their shirt, another one is looking for her hair clips, and before long *everyone is yelling*. Then you all sit in the car in silence on the way to school and work. We've all been there. Some mornings are just rough, and there's no getting around it. While getting out the door will inevitably be difficult some days, you can mitigate so much of the chaos by creating systems that allow you to have the smooth and efficient morning you deserve.

Examine the layout and space of your bedroom. Everyone has different layouts for their closets, bedrooms, and bathrooms. Perhaps you have an en suite bathroom, or maybe you need to walk down the hall to use the restroom. You may have to walk through your primary bathroom to get to your walk-in closet, or maybe you have a small reach-in closet. It's important to evaluate your space, examine your routines, and plan your organization accordingly.

The cool thing is this chapter can be applied to any bedroom or bathroom in the home, whether it be for young kids or teens. Everyone needs a system to help them function, day in and day out. But before you move to tackle someone else's room, we want you to focus on *your* space first! *You* deserve to start and end your days with a calm heart and mind—and there's no need to exert extra energy on your daily routine.

Everyone needs a system to help them function.

Have you ever walked into your space to get ready and felt an immediate wave of sadness and anxiety from all the *stuff* lying around? This should be the place full of ease and efficiency, but instead it brings stress and frustration. It doesn't have to be this way.

YOUR PERSONAL SPACE MATTERS TOO

All too often, organizing our primary bedroom closet and primary bath gets pushed to the back burner because so many of us put energy into everything and everyone *except* ourselves. Feel familiar? This is especially true if you have other people in the home who rely on you. After a long day, staring down at the pile of laundry in your bedroom chair, it's easy to tell yourself, *It's okay because no one will see it anyway.*

But *you* see it! And *you* matter!

Or maybe you convince yourself, *I'll deal with it later,* but then days turn to weeks turn to months—and the mountain of chaos just piles higher and higher. You're worth more than that!

For some of you, you may think it would be hard *not* to deal with all those piles of clutter. But for others, you know exactly what we're talking about. A pile here, a pile there, piles, piles everywhere! In our experience, more than you might realize, primary suites rarely have a well-functioning system for orderliness. The mountains of stuff (laundry, papers, returns) are real and aren't made a priority.

THE WORST WAY TO START THE DAY

Step into your bathroom and what do you see? If you're like so many others, you're likely drowning in approximately one million empty toiletry bottles on the counter. Half-used lotions and body butter. Hair-styling tools and the various dry shampoos, hair texture creams, shield sprays, and styling gels that accompany them. All the face-care products—from cleansers and toners to anti-aging creams and moisturizers. Multiple toothpaste tubes scattered in various drawers. And when you can't find the toothpaste? Open a new one. Bathrooms without a system aren't just overwhelming—they can become unhygienic quickly. If this describes you, know you're not alone.

And then, as you turn the corner, there's the primary closet. How many times have you riffled through your closet and been disappointed by how many of your clothes no longer fit? (*What a great feeling to start the day!*) Or searched for your favorite leggings, which are nowhere to be found? When your closet is cluttered with old clothes, it's increasingly difficult to find the ones you *actually* like. Plus, you have no idea what's dirty or what's clean. Shoes are mismatched and buried under a miscellaneous pile. And when you're running late, the last thing you want is to be searching all over for a missing shoe.

If you are short on closet space but you have a massive dresser, it makes sense to fold as much as you can into that piece of furniture. For dresser organization we recommend the file fold! (You can visit our Instagram to find a tutorial on this.) Whether you're placing leggings, tees, pajamas, or shorts in your dresser, if you file fold these items, you will be able to see everything you have, including your favorite logo on your favorite tee! A file fold is exactly what it sounds like: It's a fold that allows you to line your clothing items in your drawer like files in a file cabinet. You can easily sift through your clothing like hanging file folders to find what you are looking for. No more stacking items in your dresser drawers to get lost on the bottom or in the back. If

Think through small tweaks you can make to help the space work for your routines.

you get this fold down, you won't even need to place your items in a divider; each will stand on its own! But if you feel it would help provide peace of mind, a simple drawer divider will help your drawers to stay tidy!

Both in the mornings and at night, the space where you get ready should be a safe haven, not a struggle zone.

If you're not short on closet space, hang as much of your clothing as you can. T-shirts are one of those items that can either be hung or folded depending on the closet layout and space. If you have a shared bathroom down the hall from your bedroom, you might want to keep your nightly skincare items in your room so they're convenient and accessible to use when someone else is using the bathroom. If you access your closet through the bathroom, consider keeping your underwear, socks, and pajamas in a dresser in your bedroom so you can still get ready for bed even if your partner is taking a shower. Think through small tweaks you can make to help the space work for your routines.

We want you to not only experience but to truly know the sense of deep relief, calm, and even happiness that comes when your surfaces are clutter-free and your systems work for you. Getting ready is something you do every day and therefore the habits and systems you create here have a cumulative impact. There are no surprises here, so the good news is, you can create a plan that works and that supports the life you want to live. Both in the mornings and in the evenings, the space where you get ready should be a safe haven, not a struggle zone.

If you want this space to feel like the refuge you deserve, it doesn't take a ton of steps to get it there. It's finding what works for you and fits into your life. Here's what we recommend you do daily to tidy up where you get ready:

- Make your bed.
- Clear your nightstand of clutter and little bits.*
- Put away clothes (whether on a hanger or in the hamper).
- Wipe down your vanity and organize those little bits.
- Pick up any stray items on the floor.
- Turn on fans or crack a window to circulate the air.

Not everyone has a large primary suite with a his and hers walk-in closet, let alone an expansive en suite bathroom. But whether you share a bathroom with three kids or live alone, these tips are for you.

---

* You may be wondering, *What are little bits?* But you know: It's all the junk that gets sprinkled around a home, such as bobby pins, hair ties, coins, little bits of trash. We all have them. And they drive us bonkers!

TIDYING UP

WHERE YOU GET READY

BEDROOM, BATHROOM, AND CLOSET GOALS

1. Create a space that reflects your daily routines.
2. Cut down on visual clutter in your closet.
3. Reduce excess clothing.

PRODUCT LIST

- Baskets in various sizes
- Bin clips
- Hangers
- Drawer organizer bins
- Tray
- Double turntable
- Stackable drawer sets
- Divided turntables
- Lidded bins
- Label maker
- Label tape

Getting Ready Tip #1

HANG YOUR CLOTHING BY CATEGORY.

There are always a few "duh" tips in organizing, but for something that may feel obvious, this tip is often overlooked! Countless closets are full of clothing items that are just shoved in and left there without a thought. If this rings true for you, we get it—you're in a rush. But there are so many benefits to dividing and hanging your clothing items by category. By *categories*, again, think "like with like." Sleeveless tops with sleeveless tops, sweaters with sweaters, dresses with dresses, pants with pants, and so on.

The main benefit to this organizational method is that you can easily locate the item you want to wear. If you have a large, full closet, this can save you some serious time! If you want to level up, go a step further and organize each of those categories by color. This makes it even faster to zero in on that green sleeveless shirt you want to wear. Another benefit is that you can clearly see when you have too many of a certain item. Is your closet overflowing with black tank tops? Time to go through them! Use the rule "one in, one out." When you purchase a new white T-shirt, find a white T-shirt in your closet that you haven't worn in six months or more and donate it. Keep only what you actually wear.

Getting Ready Tip #2

FILL BASKETS WITH OFF-SEASON ITEMS.

Where do you store your seasonal and travel accessories? Think about all the hats, winter gear, summer gear, travel bags, and more that need a spot to live. Our favorite way to store these extra items is in baskets that can be kept at the top of the closet. Use one basket per category. Add a bin clip and label to the outside so you can easily identify each basket from where you stand. Since these are seasonal items, storing them up high makes sense. When you need your winter gear daily, simply pull down the basket to a lower spot in your closet. By using baskets to store these items, you are also cutting down on visual clutter when you open your closet door. Seeing every item you own each time you open your closet can feel overwhelming and can make you feel like you have a bigger mess on your hands than there actually is.

Getting Ready Tip #3

MANAGE ALL THE BAGS.

Whether you have a collection of purses and backpacks or store all your luggage in your closet, it's essential to decide what you actually want easily accessible. Start by identifying your favorite bags and consider using S-hooks on the clothing rod to organize them by frequency of use. For luggage, keep your weekend bags within reach at the top of the closet, while storing larger pieces in a less accessible area or a separate closet that you don't need to access regularly. This keeps your space organized and ensures you can find what you need when you need it.

Getting Ready Tip #4

UNSTUFF YOUR DRESSER.

Got a jam-packed dresser? Socks, bras, underwear, sleepwear, and workout gear often end up in a tangled mess, making it difficult to find what you're looking for when you're in a hurry. To keep things organized and easily accessible, we recommend using drawer dividers. These dividers come in various heights, so you can customize them based on the depth of your drawers. This way, you can separate workout pants from shorts, socks from bras, and undies from activewear. By dividing your items into designated sections, you'll not only save time but also create a more visually pleasing and functional drawer system, making it easier to grab exactly what you need without the chaos.

Getting Ready Tip #5

REDUCE EXCESS CLOTHING.

We all have those extra items that we simply love—vintage hand-me-downs, a kitschy holiday sweater, or a decades-old pair of jeans that reminds you of the "good ol' days." In our home, it's black concert T-shirts. Over several years, my husband ran out of space to store them, and when it was time for him to purge a few . . . *eek!* It's hard to get rid of things we love!

There are two steps in this tidying-up tip. First, tackle the items you know you have in excess—like those T-shirts. As much as you love them, there are always at least a few that can go. If you find one that's full of holes or stains, make it into a cleaning rag or just toss it. And if some are too small, donate them.

Second, if it's too difficult to part with certain excess items in your closet, then it's going to be necessary to reduce in another area of clothing. For example, if you love those shirts, but there are only a few sweaters you like to wear and your in-laws give you a new one every holiday—problem solved! Keep the shirts and donate all the sweaters you don't wear. Remember: A sentimental keep means adding something else to the donation heap. There will likely be someone else who will be delighted with the item. Keeping something in your closet out of guilt doesn't do anyone any good. Donating pays it forward.

Efficiency Tip

Keep a basket or bag on the floor of your closet for items to donate. If you try something on and hate how it looks or feels, toss it in the basket. When the basket is full, it's time for a donation drop-off!

Getting Ready Tip #6

STORE DAILY-USE PRODUCTS AT THE TOP OF YOUR BATHROOM VANITY.

There are a lot of items to be stored in a bathroom vanity: hair products, face care, lotions, nail care, dental care, and the list goes on. Be deliberate with how you divide the space and store each category.

The first step when organizing a bathroom is to pull all daily-use products and store them in a top drawer of the vanity. We want these things to be easy to reach every day. Daily-use items include deodorant, toothbrush, toothpaste, lip balm, floss, and contacts—any item that would be annoying to have to bend down for two times a day, every day. Consider lining the drawer with drawer organizer bins, and remember: Keep like with like. Each bin holds its own separate category. (Extra points for labeling it!) We like to use the other bathroom drawers for hair tools, hair accessories, feminine products, washcloths, and travel toiletries. But if you lack drawer space, bring in a double turntable or tray to store your most-used items on top of the vanity.

Getting Ready Tip #7

USE THE UNDER-SINK VERTICAL SPACE.

Open the cabinet under your bathroom sink and take a look. Are you using only the space at the very bottom? If the answer is yes, don't worry—most people are doing the same! Bathroom cabinets are typically quite big, and most vanities don't come with shelves inside due to plumbing requirements. That leaves us with a lot of wasted real estate under there. And this is a *great* place for less-used items to live.

Just like in your laundry room, maximize your storage by using your vertical space well. Bring in small stackable drawers for under the sink. Just think about all those extra inches! Another under-sink favorite of ours is a divided turntable. The divided sections can store hair care, lotions, facial products, and nail care by categories. You can even add labels to each section!

Since under-sinks can be such a vast storage spot, storing hair tools under the sink is a great solution! Whether you're using a long bin or an over-the-door caddy on the cabinet door for hair tools, you can easily roll your cords tight and have plenty of room for hair tools galore!

Getting Ready Tip #8

STORE BACK-STOCK ITEMS IN ANOTHER SPOT.

With warehouse stores growing in popularity, in addition to our online autoship and subscription options, it's likely that your back-stock collection is growing too. Buying in bulk is a great cost-saving method, but it does require some creative thinking when it comes to storage. Really, no matter how big a bathroom is, there rarely is enough storage for all your current products plus their backups.

Instead, create back-stock bins to store your extra items. Choose one category per bin and label the outside. One for shaving, one for dental care, one for deodorants or toiletries—you get the idea. Use lidded bins so you can stack them if needed and place them at the top of your linen closet or even the top of your clothing closet. When it's time for a new shaving cream, you'll know exactly where to go. This system helps you gain space in your bathroom, which may have been bursting at the seams before.

Getting Ready Tip #9

CUT DOWN ON WASHCLOTHS AND TOWELS.

Do you still have the towels you bought during your first year of college? Or the towels you received as a wedding shower gift? If some time has passed since then, it's time to revise your collection. Chances are, you've added newer washcloths, hand towels, and body towels since then and have also kept the older ones. If you do laundry regularly, you really don't need more than two or three towels per family member. (For a two-person household, we recommend keeping four to six towels.)

We do want you to have some towels on hand that you don't mind getting stained. In chapter 1 we suggested that you store these in the laundry room instead of in your bathroom, though, so the cleanup towels don't get confused with your regular towels. No one will be happy if the babysitter grabs your nice, white, fluffy towels to soak up grape juice that spilled on the floor or for cleaning Rover's muddy paws!

LEVEL UP WHERE YOU GET READY

Match your hangers. We want to make this clear: There is absolutely nothing wrong with having a closet full of mismatched hangers. They're getting the job done. So updating to matching hangers can seem like a superfluous choice to make for some, but having matching hangers can cut down on the visual clutter of your closet and can help keep the hooks from getting tangled. It's a minor detail that can make a big difference. If your clothing rod is full of hangers in multiple colors, your closet can seem more chaotic than it actually is.

Switching to matching hangers can be a bit of an investment. A great idea is to buy one new pack at a time, especially if you have a lot of clothes. When you get a new pack of hangers, switch them out that day. When the next month rolls around, rinse and repeat. Switching out all your hangers in one setting can be quite an arm workout. It's harder than you would think! Whether you do it all at once or over the course of a few months, seeing a clothing rod with all matching hangers not only looks nice; it feels tidier.

Redesign! Oh man, do we have a leveling-up tip for you! This will require time and patience but can make an enormous difference. Whether you have wire shelving or something even older, if you want to elevate your closet space, *design a new one!* This can seem daunting, but there are a lot of simple options to get you started.

Many companies have online portals to enter closet measurements, and then they design a custom system for your needs. In addition to the DIY options, you can also hire a company to measure and install a closet system. We love customizing closets for our clients because it gives them a unique space that they love and want to maintain.

SQUARE FOOTAGE PROBLEMS?

Optimize nooks and crannies. It can be tricky to come up with unique solutions for small closets, bedrooms, and bathrooms. We find that the tinier the closet, the more our client loves fashion! Even if that's the case, there are many apartment-friendly options that add more space for all your pretty things. We like to add shoe storage to the backs of closet doors, under-bed storage bins for sweaters, and shelf risers or additional shelving to use the full height of the closet, allowing you to store anything seasonal and offering you more space. When you're tight on space, remember the goal isn't to tuck things out of the way and forget about them; instead, it's more about being intentional with the size of the space you have and knowing exactly what you can fit there so nothing is lost or forgotten.

MANTRA

An emotional keep means adding something else to the donation heap.

Chapter Six

TIDYING UP WHERE YOU SLEEP

This is our favorite part of the home! We love rest. The end. But seriously, what chapter is more fitting to follow tidying up where you get ready? If you've already tackled the major issues of the primary "getting ready" spaces—the bathroom, closets, and the rest of the bedroom—there is still more to do that will help you tidy up where you sleep. As we mentioned before, the bedroom should be a safe haven, a place that allows you to feel relaxed and at ease. Tidying up this area is so important in reducing stress.[1] What we share here can be applied to guest bedrooms and kiddos' bedrooms too!

Getting your bedroom organized is about far more than just aesthetics. This also affects your mental wellness.[2] When your space is clutter-free, it's easier to unwind, which can help you sleep much better, creating a positive cycle of reinforcement. This space is all

> **This space is all about nurturing your mind so you can feel calm and let go of the day.**

about nurturing your mind so you can feel calm and let go of the day—which then helps you get ready to start the next one well.

You know what makes rest difficult to achieve? Clothes strewn across the room, piles of old mail, and cords lying all around the nightstand. Books askew on every flat surface, random kid toys sprinkled around, and sheets bundled at the floor of the unmade bed. Nightstands are filled to the brim, laundry baskets are piled high, and paperwork is spewing out from under the bed.

It's impossible to truly rest in this kind of environment.

Tidying up around your bed takes dedicated focus because this is often a trap where random stuff accumulates. It's time-consuming to go through all the piles and extra chargers. And most important, it's crucial to match bed linens and ensure you're tossing any that have holes and stains.

This is time well invested. Once you conquer these cluttered, catchall spaces and choose to include only the items you love, you can come back to your room and actually relax. No more screaming piles of stuff. No more endless to-dos. Bedrooms become sanctuaries, and that's what we want for you.

Again, an orderly bedroom can contribute to better mental health: Clutter can be overwhelming and can make it difficult to relax.[3] By creating an organized sleeping environment, you can foster a sense of control and accomplishment, which can positively affect your mood and mental clarity.[4] Taking the time to arrange your space thoughtfully allows you to create a personal haven that supports your well-being, ultimately helping you feel more balanced and centered in other areas of your life.

An orderly bedroom can contribute to better mental health.

When we talk about tidying up where you sleep, we want you to home in on what makes you feel the most calm and relaxed. Is it nice sheets with high thread count? A cute lamp? A great book to read? Always having your glasses within arm's reach? Maybe you like a weighted blanket or need a white noise machine nearby. Whatever it is, our tips will help you keep where you sleep tidy. You'll still have what you need, and the items you *don't* need will have a home elsewhere.

REST YOUR MIND

You might be tempted to think, *It's just a bedroom; no one will see it, right?* But the person who pays the price for a messy room is you! When you don't make your own space a priority, it leads to feelings of stress, overwhelm, and a lack of control that you carry with you throughout your day.[5] That feeling of overwhelm can bleed into your relationships at home or at work.[6] How you start and end your day matters for your personal wellness, and your bedroom chaos prevents the peace and confidence you crave.

Many of us know that sensation of calm after we spend some time tidying up our rooms. It's empowering when you take control of your personal space. You deserve a bedroom that feels safe. A place where you can feel good and calm. A place of rest and intimacy. A place that oozes coziness.

How can you achieve this sense of peace? It starts with being intentional about what you allow in your most private and personal space in the home. This requires minimizing distractions and visual clutter. From waking up to walking out the door for the day, we want you to feel confident and at ease. But it's difficult to relax if you see papers and piles cluttering your dresser or stacks of items to return packaged on the floor—constant reminders of your never-ending to-do list. Each piece of clutter is a reminder of *something else* you need to do. That constant feeling of "should" stands in the way of your peace.

The bedroom should be your sanctuary—a place to recharge, both physically and mentally.

Creating a peaceful, organized bedroom isn't just about aesthetics; it's about setting the tone for both your day and night. When any space is cluttered, your mind becomes cluttered too—and it could be argued that your sleeping space is, therefore, the most important to have clear and organized. The constant visual reminders of unfinished tasks, stray items, and piles of things waiting to be dealt with can drain your mental energy as you go to sleep and then again before you even begin your day. The bedroom should be your sanctuary—a place to recharge, both physically and mentally. When you prioritize tidying up this space, you're investing in your overall well-being. A clean, calm environment helps you feel more in control, centered, and ready to tackle what's next.

Another benefit of keeping your bedroom tidy is the opportunity to reconnect with what truly matters to you. Think about the items that bring you peace or harmony in this space. Is it your favorite blanket? The world's softest set of sheets? A cherished photo? When you clear the clutter, you create space and clear visibility to bring these meaningful items into focus. A thoughtful approach to organization allows you to surround yourself with what nurtures you while letting go of things that no longer serve you. The goal is not perfection, but intentionality. A well-organized bedroom doesn't just help you sleep better—it empowers you to *live* better. It's a place where you can let go of the day, recharge, and feel ready to embrace the next one with clarity and calm.

TIDYING UP
WHERE YOU SLEEP

BEDROOM GOALS

1. Identify what needs (and doesn't need) to live in your bedroom.
2. Bring in bedside storage.
3. Revise bed linens.

PRODUCT LIST

- Nightstands with drawers
- Drawer organizers in various sizes
- Museum gel
- Charging station
- Small hampers
- Baskets in various sizes
- Lamps
- Label maker
- Label tape

Sleep Tip #1

IDENTIFY WHAT HELPS YOU SLEEP WELL.

For us, it's a comfy bed, a phone charger, a good book, nighttime medications, lip balm, and a white noise machine. Keep only those items that promote rest and relaxation in your sleeping space. To do this, determine exactly—and only—what you need. Deciding what should be close to you at night and in the morning helps to clarify what does, and does *not*, need to live in your bedroom.

One of the main goals in organizing the space where you sleep is to take away the items that cause you more stress and anxiety. We've already mentioned how bedrooms often become a catchall space.

So if that pile of laundry makes you feel anxious, let's find another spot to fold it. If you have important documents like birth certificates and car titles shoved into your nightstand and feel low-grade anxiety every time you see them, let's pull them out. Bring in a firesafe file box to keep them in and store it in the closet or home office. If seeing paperwork stacked next to your bed causes you stress, eliminate work from the bedroom. Even if you think these things don't bother you, we invite you to experiment with keeping only essentials in your bedroom. You might be surprised how much better you sleep.

Sleep Tip #2

BRING IN A NIGHTSTAND WITH DRAWERS.

We've seen our fair share of bedrooms without nightstands or with nightstands that lack any type of storage and end up collecting clutter. Don't let your nightstand surface become a default storage spot! If your nightstand is loaded down with a glass of water, phone, charging cords, a few books, hair ties, random pens, a journal, your nighttime moisturizer, some loose change, earbuds, a Kindle, and all the other items you use as you unwind at night—it's time to find each of those items its own home. Otherwise, in little to no time, it's going to get crazy again! That's the exact *opposite* of the calm and serene environment you are trying to create.

In our opinion, not having a workable nightstand is a real missed opportunity. We suggest bringing in a nightstand (or two, if you live with a partner) that has at least two to three drawers. This will be adequate storage for your daily and nightly items plus some other things that make sense being stored bedside—such as heating pads, journals, tissues, extra chargers, and flashlights.

Sleep Tip #3

USE DRAWER ORGANIZERS FOR THE NIGHTSTAND.

Once you have a nightstand with adequate storage, it's time to establish a maintainable system so that your necessities always have a home. This means there's always a place for them to be tucked away, and unnecessary items don't make their way in.

To set up an easily maintainable system in a nightstand, bring in an assortment of small drawer organizers with straight sides. (Remember, no tapered sides.) Empty out the drawer completely and line it with different-sized organizers so the entire space is filled. You might be left with some open space at the edges, but we will take care of that by using a product called museum gel. Museum gel can be purchased online and is a clear adhesive you can use on the bottom of each organizer to keep it from moving around. Divide your drawer contents into categories: daily medications, lip care, lotions, hair bands, glasses, and whatever other daily items you want beside your bed. Place each category into its own bin and add a label to the side of each one. When you need your hand lotion, you know right where it is. And better yet? After putting it back in its place, you'll know exactly where it is for the next night too.

Sleep Tip #4

CREATE EASY CHARGING SOLUTIONS.

We all own so many devices these days, each one requiring a different charging cord. I charge my phone, watch, earbuds, and tablet daily. That means four separate cords running to my night-stand. Talk about an eyesore, not to mention a safety hazard. If you double that cord count to include your partner's devices, the two of you have a *lot* of chargers. When you have cords running all over, the room can feel messy even when the bed is made and the laundry is put away. Those cords quickly become visual clutter.

To streamline your charging setup, we suggest bringing in a multipurpose charging station. This is one device with one power cord that can charge all the things! In addition to cutting down on cord clutter, it also clears up the top of your nightstand. Some nightstands have a top drawer that has been converted into a charging center with cords running down the back of the piece of furniture. We love this even more since it cuts way down on the visual mess.

Sleep Tip #5

EXCHANGE A LARGE HAMPER FOR A SMALLER ONE.

This might seem counterintuitive, but hear us out. Most people wait to do the laundry until the basket or hamper is full to overflowing. So when laundry baskets are large, this means you'll have multiple loads of washing, drying, and folding in front of you. But with smaller hampers, laundry is done more often, is more manageable, *and* the basket doesn't take up as much space.

Consider keeping a small laundry basket for every person in your home and keep your loads separate when doing laundry. This way, there's no time wasted sorting the clothes for each person before putting them away. Plus, when the kids are old enough, they can wash their own laundry themselves—even better!

Sleep Tip #6

REDUCE YOUR BED LINENS.

You wouldn't believe the volume contained in some linen collections. If you have decades' worth of top sheets, fitted sheets, pillowcases, and blankets, it might be time to let some go. When people pare down their belongings, linens rarely top that list, so no judgment. But linens are actually a great place to tidy up because they take up so much space.

Start by ridding your closet of the sheets with holes or stains. Next, sort the sets by size (king, queen, double, or twin). Just like a piece of Tupperware without a lid, search for any sheets without a mate. One flat sheet without a matching fitted sheet? Get rid of it.

So how many do you really need? We suggest keeping two sets per bed. If you have one king-sized bed, two queen-sized beds, and one twin, it's okay to keep two king sheet sets, four queen sheet sets, and two twin sheet sets. But that should be it. The one exception is if you own an air mattress. You may want to keep one extra set for that. For comforters and duvets, keep one extra per bed—and that's only if you switch them out seasonally, such as using a heavier one for winter and a cooler one for summer.

Pillows are another item that can get out of hand quickly. At most, keep one extra pillow per bed in your home. If you have three beds, keep three extra pillows. This should be plenty in case your guests prefer a different type or if you want to have some extra on hand to use with the air mattress.

Sleep Tip #7

KEEP EACH ROOM'S BED LINENS IN THAT ROOM.

Because we suggest keeping only two sheet sets per bed, one will be on the bed and the other can be stored in the same bedroom. The set that's not being used can be in a basket in the closet or in a dresser drawer or in a storage bench. Of course, we suggest labeling the basket or drawer with the sheet size so everyone in the home (including house cleaners, if you have them) is aware of the system. We like to have clients do this for kids' rooms and guest rooms too. This makes keeping up with the different-sized sets so much easier. Instead of digging through your linen closet to find a king-sized fitted sheet, flat sheet, and set of pillowcases when you're changing sheets—let alone in the middle of the night because your sweet pup or child had an accident—you can just walk over to the basket in your closet and grab the extra set. Doesn't that sound easy?

Sleep Tip #8

FIND A BASKET FOR CURRENT READING MATERIAL.

If you're a big reader, we know how fast the bedside area can become piled high with books. There's the pile of books you want to read, the books you are currently reading, and the books you just read. It can get out of hand quickly.

Create a habit of taking your completed reads out of your room. If you want to keep them, add them to your bookshelf. If you want to pass them to a friend, have a bag designated for this purpose and grab it the next time you two visit. If they are library books, return them—you don't want that fine!

Now you're left with your to-be-read and currently reading stacks, which we love to keep in a basket close to the bed. This gives a clear visual boundary to refrain from bringing in any more material if the basket is full. The goal is to work through your current stack before adding to it. If you notice your basket looks empty, it's time for a trip to the library or bookstore! How fun!

Sleep Tip #9

USE LAMPS FOR AMBIENT LIGHTING.

One of the goals in your bedroom is to make it calm and cozy so you can feel relaxed and at peace. Harsh overhead lighting creates the opposite effect. Generally speaking, we're not big fans of overhead lights throughout the home, but this is especially true in the bedroom. They're just so bright and intrusive. Of course they have their purpose, but for most of the time, what you really need is some cozy lighting. Enter lamps. We will never be mad at a matching pair of lamps for your nightstands. It's a fun way to bring some color, texture, and personality into the space. By turning off the overhead light and bringing in beautiful lamps next to the bed, you are upping your cozy factor by a thousand percent!

Pro tip: A warm-colored bulb is inviting and relaxing whereas a bright white-colored bulb is energizing. This is important to remember when purchasing light bulbs for each room.

LEVEL UP WHERE YOU SLEEP

Invest in the space. So many bedrooms are full of hand-me-down furniture. A lot of people think, *No one comes into my bedroom. Why does it matter?* But *you* matter, and of any space in your home, this place should feel most like you. Elevate your bedroom with new nightstands and, if possible, a new dresser. For us, personally, the bedroom is our favorite room, and we've loved making ours our own. A dresser can be a statement piece of mid-century beauty, but it also has many drawers for storage.

If you have a larger bedroom, you can organize and maximize the space in a way that allows you to enjoy it even more. For some, that might mean setting up a cozy reading nook, or maybe you love knitting or another calming activity. Less clutter overall means more room for what makes you happy. Tidying up where you sleep can transform this space into a more functional, enjoyable, and inspiring area.

SQUARE FOOTAGE PROBLEMS?

Get down-under storage. These days you can find many beds with built-in storage underneath—a great idea when space is an issue. In addition to drawers, the mattress platform itself can lift up, creating more room to store items you rarely use like luggage, extra bedding, and seasonal items. Using the under-bed storage space frees up other areas for things you want to access more often. Win-win!

MANTRA

Keep only what you need to sleep.

Chapter Seven

TIDYING UP WHERE YOU PLAY

When you have kiddos, you quickly realize how easily their stuff ends up anywhere and everywhere, especially if you don't have one designated spot for all of it. And we want to help. This chapter will be kid-specific, so feel free to skip ahead if you're not dealing with millions of little toys. But if this is you, awash in a sea of playthings, read on, my friend.

Think about the space in your home where you want most of the toys and kid items to live. We know a lot of people who don't want any toys in the child's bedroom, while others purposely choose to have play areas in multiple rooms. It just depends on what the kids are into, where they prefer to play, and what you're comfortable with based on various factors. No matter what you decide, all toys need a home. This will look different for each of

Overall, a tidy play area makes the whole family happy.

you, depending on the layout of your home and your needs at this stage of life.

For instance, we've seen home offices that incorporate a small zone with toys for a little one to play in. We've also seen a ton of living rooms full to the brim of every toy imaginable, simply because the kids want to be close to mom and dad while they're playing. It's also common for guest rooms to flex as a space for play, as well as basements, where you can practically toss toys down there and the kids can run amok and have their own little haven of adventure. And if you happen to have a whole room dedicated as a playroom, that's wonderful!

For us, we've had to learn to embrace the term *multipurpose room* when it comes to our kids' toys. Plus, we want our kids to play and learn independently. This is good for their development, *and* it gives us more time to get things done at home!

No matter your situation, creating a system for toys, books, and activities is one of the best things you can do for your home. You can establish systems that allow both you and your kiddos to thrive. Mom, Dad, kids, and caregivers should know where things are and where they should be put back. We'll help you create a system so everyone can pitch in and keep up. Overall, a tidy play area makes the whole family happy.

CREATING A SYSTEM THAT WORKS

So how can you create a system that allows your child to easily find the toy they want to play with, while also concealing these toys from view? Our main advice for this space right up front is not to be afraid to reduce your items.

Or if you're able to stay on top of it, try toy rotation. Keep some toys out for everyday play, and tuck away the rest in a storage bin kept in a closet. After a few weeks, switch them out. This system helps keep the home tidy and simplified, while also keeping your child engaged. Plus, there's no real reason to have *every* toy out and on display all the time. And for those that are rarely played with, pulling items out of rotation for a bit can be a great way to extend a toy's play-life.

Keep in mind: Remember that overwhelm you feel from visual clutter? Kids experience that too! When all the toys are out and it's hard to see individual items, it's easy for them to dismiss all of them and not find anything they want to play with. If you were a kid, would you want to sort through a mess just to *maybe* find one thing you wanted to play with? Probably not. And as frustrating as it can be when your kids have a hard time playing independently, think about how a bit of effort up front on your part can help them toward that goal. Kids love simple things! How much fun do they have with big empty boxes? Or pots and pans when they're little? There's a complete *lack* of complexity with those things. These items are straightforward, and kids can be as creative as they want. We're not implying that we want you to have only cardboard lying around your playroom. But it's important to realize simplicity is key in play spaces. If you've ever said, "They have so many toys but don't seem to really play with any of them," this strategy is for you!

GETTING STARTED

But how do you begin to create a system to organize these toys and supplies? This can get tricky because there are so many different categories and subcategories in any given play space. If you have kiddos across different age ranges, there are even more categories to consider—board books or chapter books, a five-piece wooden puzzle or a thousand-piece set, soft toys or action figures. And then, there are the stuffed animals. They come in so many different shapes and sizes, they range across all groups, and they're all so *special*, it's hard to know what to do with them all. Each household will need an individualized system for toys, but one thing stays true: Group "like with like."

The benefits of dedicating a space on the main level of your home is that you can keep a close eye on your kids while they play. But these spaces are often some of the first rooms guests see when entering the house. *Eek!* That's a scary thought! If this sounds like your situation, we suggest considering how you can use closed storage pieces, something with doors that can be shut when you are expecting guests over. Or shelves with baskets or fabric bins that match your decor. These are better choices than having all the toys out in the open.

Sometimes an extra bedroom or a bonus room is converted into a playroom. This is great for the never-ending toy mess, but not so great for being able to monitor little ones when you're in another part of the house, like while you're cooking dinner or working from the kitchen table. If the kids entertain themselves for the most part, make everything accessible for them that they might want or need, *except* for the items that need more supervision. (For us, that's playdough, paint, glitter, and tiny toys.)

As you begin to think about tidying up your play space, here's a list of categories that might help you organize your storage:

- Action figures
- Animals
- Baby doll accessories
- Baby dolls
- Balls
- Barbie accessories
- Barbies
- Blocks
- Board games
- Dress up/pretend play
- Magnetic tiles
- Musical instruments
- Play kitchen
- Puzzles
- Stuffies
- Vehicles

For crafts, these are the most common categories:

- Activity books
- Coloring books
- Crayons
- Glue
- Markers
- Miscellaneous craft supplies (popsicle sticks, feathers, glitter—*noooo!*)
- Paint
- Paintbrushes
- Paper
- Scissors
- Stickers
- Tape

As toys change, your systems will too.

Inevitably, as your child's tastes change and toys fall out of favor, you'll want to donate unused toys to a local charity or give them to a friend. And as toys change, your systems will too. Don't wait until the bins are overflowing with too many toys. Revisit your child's toys, books, and craft supplies approximately every six months. Use these moments to reconsider if your storage systems still apply to your child's tastes, and if not, develop new ones.

TIDYING UP

WHERE YOU PLAY

PLAY AREA GOALS

1. Determine what type of play you want to encourage in this space.
2. Reduce and donate from the toys, books, and crafts collection.
3. Label everything, so both kids and adults know where everything goes.

PRODUCT LIST

- Clear narrow bins
- Cube organizer
- Large baskets
- Wire hampers
- Photo ledges
- Over-the-door organizer
- Tiered rolling cart
- Garment rack
- Kid hangers
- Label maker
- Label tape

Play Tip #1

EVALUATE THE SPACE AND DECIDE ON ITS FUNCTION.

Not many homes come with a designated playroom, unless it has been custom-built with young ones in mind. In many homes, a never-used dining room or office is converted into a playroom. And there are a lot of us who must embrace that multipurpose idea—doubling a living room, guest room, or basement as a playroom. The setup for how you store your kids' toys will look different depending on your space, the ages of your kids, and the types of play they engage in. You get to decide what types of objects you want to bring into your home and how you want your space to be used.

Play Tip #2

DONATE!

If you have kids, you know how often new toys enter your home. It can seem like new ones pop up weekly with all the birthdays, holidays, and YouTube videos influencing your little ones. It's important to go through toy collections every six months. Donate toys that haven't been played with or that your children have outgrown. It's also a good idea to toss toys that are broken or are missing parts. Because let's be real: How often do you actually glue back the arm of the small action figure guy? For me, it's never. And how often do your kids play with toy sets that are missing several pieces? Probably very seldom.

Just like how other rooms in your home can cause anxiety when filled with too much stuff, the same is true for kids. If the play space houses every single toy that has ever been purchased for them since birth, they may not be able to articulate it, but they can feel overwhelmed by *so much stuff*. This reminds us of how women look in their closets packed full of clothes and think, *I have nothing to wear*. Revision helps everyone see what they have and use what they own. When there's too much to see, too much to step over, and too much input, kids have a hard time making a choice. Streamlining a play space is so important. You want your kids to feel inspired and imaginative in the room—*not* overcome with indecision.

Play Tip #3

SELECT SMALL CLEAR BINS TO DIVIDE UP TOYS.

Bins are the easiest way to make toys accessible for play *and* are easy to clean up—the dream team of the playroom universe! After you have revised the toy collection, by ditching any broken items and donating the never-played-with items, it's time to divide the remaining toys by category. We suggest getting specific with the categories as we listed on page 145 (and feel free to add your own!). We love to bring stackable, clear, narrow bins into play spaces and organize each category into its own bin. If you have a category that's overflowing, bring in a larger bin or divide it in two. Storing toys in clear bins makes it easy for kids to find exactly what they're looking for. And kids are so smart! Even if they can't read a label, they can scan the bins and understand the system: like with like. This is how most classrooms are set up, so why not do it at home as well? And when it's time to clean up, just pull the right bin over and encourage your little one to help you put it all back. Eventually, they will be independent enough to do it "all by myself."

Play Tip #4

USE CUBES.

You've already divided every little toy into a small bin, so now what in the world are you to do with all those bins? We like using the cube organizers that you can get from any big-box retailer, the ones that come configured with six or eight open square shelves.

We love these because they make play so easy for little ones. When the storage cube is placed horizontally, every shelf is low to the ground for easy access—so important in a play space. If you have straight (nontapered) bins, two to four of the narrow ones can fit in each open cube—and they can be stacked! We love this setup if your kids can entertain themselves. This system makes playtime *and* cleanup easy and accessible. If you're setting up a playroom or play area that's more visible to the rest of the house, and those toys don't quite go with your decor, consider adding doors to the cube organizer. Another option is to bring in a low-profile storage piece that comes with cabinet doors so you can line the bins up inside. When you have people over, just shut the cabinet doors and no one sees the millions of toys hiding inside!

Play Tip #5

FIND BIG BASKETS FOR STUFFED ANIMALS.

My kids *love* stuffed animals. But they are the bane of my existence—they take up *so much space*! We've found that it's hard to store stuffies, mostly because they come in so many different shapes and sizes. Not to mention how difficult it is to handle the tricky hierarchy. Some are just loved more than others! But that's a great way to sort them. We ranked them in three categories: the stuffed animals with the most importance—the ones our kiddos must have to go to sleep every night and that stay on the bed (tier one), and the least important—ones kept solely for an emotional connection or as a memento, which should be moved to a memento bin (tier three).

That just leaves managing the ones they like to play with fairly often: tier two. We like to bring in a big basket or see-through hamper to store this category. You'd be surprised by how many stuffed animals you can fit in one basket. Store these baskets around the playroom or in the bottom of your child's bedroom closet. Anything that doesn't fall into those three categories should be donated.

Play Tip #6

KEEP CRAFT SUPPLIES SAFE.

We *love* creativity and encourage it as much and as often as possible. But does any parent want kids to have access to *all* the art supplies *all* the time? The markers might not need to be within arm's reach of the three-year-old—just saying! Each child has a different capacity and interest in crafting. What you need to keep accessible will determine the size and amount of space to designate for storage. If your kiddo loves Play-Doh and stickers, put them up where you can get them down for your kids, not in a place where they can sticker up your front window and grind dough into the carpet. As kids age, their ability to enjoy craft supplies independently grows.

Play Tip #7

HANG A LEDGE OR SHELF FOR BOOKS AND PUZZLES.

There are so many fun, beautiful, and creative books and puzzles for kids, it's hard to pass them up. They make great gifts for baby showers and birthdays, too, so it's easy to find yourself with quite a collection. But just like with toys and stuffed animals, it's important to go through these and update them every six months to a year.

Donate or regift books that have been outgrown by your children, or pass them down to younger friends or cousins. We understand that some books bring back wonderful memories for you and your kiddos, and it's okay to keep a few for sentimental reasons—just store them in a memento bin, not on your current shelf. It's also okay to toss puzzles that are missing pieces, since chances are they will no longer be played with.

We suggest adding photo ledges or book rails to the lower parts of walls in playrooms. Place books and puzzles on the ledges and lean them against the wall so they're visible and easy to grab. This will also add a fun pop of color to the room!

Play Tip #8

ADD LABELS TO EVERY BIN AND BASKET.

This is probably the single most important part of a playroom setup. Why? Because this system will be maintainable over many years and can be adjusted as your kids get older. Labels not only help kids maintain the playroom setup, but they help the parents and caregivers too. If your child doesn't read yet? No problem. Add labels with the names of the items *and* include a clip art image. This system will help keep the playroom tidy and can be one more place to encourage kids when they're learning to read.

Most of the label makers available today have a wide range of clip art images to choose from. Just like when we suggested you get specific when dividing the categories, we also suggest you get specific when creating the labels. For instance, when organizing a Barbie collection, create a bin for the Barbie dolls, a bin for the Barbie clothes, and a bin for the Barbie accessories. And use those category names to label each bin. It sounds like it might make cleaning up more tedious, but we've found the exact opposite to be true. In our experience, kids play better and longer when the toys are easy to see and not all jumbled together. So even if, at first, you find this setup time-consuming, you'll find it pays off with more independent play in the long run.

Play Tip #9

USE AN OVER-THE-DOOR ORGANIZER OR TIERED CART FOR ART SUPPLIES.

Over-the-door organizers are a great way to manage all the various arts and crafts supplies! And when you feel your child can be responsible accessing these supplies anytime, then you might be ready to trust them with an art cart.

The thought of giving kids free rein with paint and glitter in a carpeted room—or any room really—makes us feel nauseated. We can't be the only ones who hesitate to store arts and crafts supplies in the playroom. Many of us prefer to keep crafts near the kitchen table instead, just in case a big mess happens. This way, we can be close by to intervene.

Choose the best place to complete crafts in your home and then find a nearby playroom or closet door where you can store all the art supplies. Then get yourself an over-the-door organizer with baskets. Place the least messy supplies—the ones you don't mind the kiddos having direct access to at all times—on the bottom. Reserve the ones with the potential for the biggest messes at the top, where only an adult can reach. We tuck paint, glitter, Play-Doh, slime, markers, and beads up there, so the kids have to ask for these items. With this system, you'll always know when a Sharpie is being used—no surprise permanent artwork!

Play Tip #10

SET UP A GARMENT RACK FOR COSTUMES.

Do you have any costume-loving littles? After a great day of dressing up as princesses or superheroes or animals, where do those costumes go? Oftentimes, they're shoved together in a big bin, meaning the ones at the bottom never get worn. Or even worse, your child might dump out the entire bin just to find the little glove they wanted.

If this sounds familiar, try incorporating a small garment rack into your play space. Many stores sell garment racks that can be adjusted to child height. Grab a pack of kid-sized hangers and hang every costume in your home. You can also use bins to line the bottom of the rack and store smaller accessories like wands, shoes, masks, hats, and so on. Just like with other areas of the play space, if your kiddos can easily see their costumes, they are more likely to play with them. We suggest not overstuffing the rack. You want to keep the choices to a minimum so it's not overwhelming. Just like other categories in this chapter, go through the costumes every six months and donate the ones that no longer fit or are no longer in use.

LEVEL UP WHERE YOU PLAY

Build it in. We've mentioned that the play space is one of our favorite spots in the home to organize; we just love coming up with all sorts of storage solutions for busy families! But after we've sorted and revised all the toys, we also work with clients to design a play space with brand-new shelving and cabinets that maximize space. Built-ins not only look great, but can evolve with your kids' needs as they grow older.

SQUARE FOOTAGE PROBLEMS?

Use under-bed space. Small houses or apartments usually have just as much kid stuff as bigger homes do, which can make things tight. Sometimes kids share a room, too, which means working around multiple beds, different sizes of clothing, books of varyious reading levels, and all the toys. The key is to use every nook—especially the space under the beds—to store toys and stuffed animals. Think of this as bonus square footage! Don't just shove stuff under there in a rush; be intentional about it! Purchase some lidded, plastic under-the-bed bins. Usually, four will fit under each bed. Place each kiddo's toys there, and just like we mentioned earlier, create a labeled system. Dolls and Barbies in one bin, costumes in another, puzzles and games in another, and stuffed animals in the final one. Or organize into whichever categories of toys your kiddos love. Keep like with like! By creating a system for toys, even in a small space, you can gain quite a bit of functional storage.

MANTRA

Revise, rotate, donate, play!

Chapter Eight

TIDYING UP WHERE YOU WORK

Both of us started to work from home after our first kids were born. And wow, it's tricky! There's just so much inherent distraction at home. When household tasks are in view, it becomes a struggle to stay focused.

Whether you're in a large home or a small apartment, whether you share your space or live alone—no matter what, you need a space where you can focus. A place that allows you to excel at your job with confidence and efficiency. The main problem we see most often in workspaces, though, is that it becomes a catch-all space—even worse than a junk drawer! It's tempting to add *all* your to-dos to this space—your return pile, gifted art from the kids' school, paperwork from three years ago, home decor you'd like to sell. Surrounded by all this clutter, it's difficult to know which task to begin first. Not to mention that if it's cluttered, you may not even

> **If there's no system in place, it can be difficult to find motivation to start your work every morning.**

be able to physically sit down and use your space to get to the tasks at hand.

The fact of the matter is, you likely have a lot to do. No one else can manage those emails or attend that meeting in your place. No one else can call the car insurance company for you, and no one else can review and file those school papers. These are things you need to deal with, but not all at once. What we're after in this space is *focus*, and a well-functioning office with simple systems can give you that. If there's no system in place, it can be difficult to find motivation to start your work every morning.

MAKE IT WORK

We've seen a lot of different workspace concepts in our clients' homes: a dedicated office room; a "cloffice" (closet/office) or a desk tucked against a wall of another space, like the kitchen or a bedroom. And the good news is, all these options can work great! No matter what kind of workspace you have, it's crucial that you create a functional and distraction-free zone: a place where you can focus on your intended task at hand. A place that minimizes distractions. A place that supports what you're aiming to achieve.

If your office doesn't feel inviting or functional for you, you may feel tempted to escape to a couch or crawl into bed while you send emails. This isn't great for productivity—or posture, for that matter.

Plus, when you lack a designated workspace and blur the lines between your desk chair and your couch, you rob yourself of the protective boundaries you deserve. Creating a designated workspace is crucial for your mental wellness because it separates your work from the rest of your life.[1] Boundaries can be as simple as shutting down or closing your computer for the day, so you know your work time is over and you can go spend time with your family. Turning off the light in your office space, or shutting a door if you have one, can signal that you're now "closed for the day." These physical cues are so important to tell your brain that work is done, and you can now center yourself into personal time (and not be tempted to go check on work again). It's easy to find our way back to work when we're stressed or bored, which is why these boundaries are important.

WORKSPACES VERSUS WORKSHOPS

The bulk of the tips in this chapter are catered to traditional office spaces in the home for those with a "desk job." But if your work zone is a creative space—like an art studio or a workshop in your garage—these tips can still apply, especially if you have huge projects to work on. As creators ourselves, we know how easy it is to get distracted while creating, as well as how many supplies we like to always have around. We can easily fall into the trap of justifying our messy behavior with statements like "I'm just an artist." But we don't want a messy space to be the default.

While these creative spaces don't need to be perfect, they should have some order for you to be able to thrive in.

In the past I've had a whole room as my personal studio; then I grew it to three rooms to store art, to store supplies, and to create. Now I'm down to one tiny wall in my basement! I've had to learn how to reorganize my supplies, knowing what I need to keep and where, no matter my circumstances. Having a tidy workspace helps me create more art, which helps me feel so joyful and fulfilled!

These same ideas can be applied to workspaces that are more functional or physical in nature. We grew up with uncles and grandfathers who had garages to tinker in (or disappear into), and we think it's great to have this type of work zone (says the lady with the small art studio). A workshop thrives on tidiness, but it's a space you can be a little more laid back with. It's not an area everyone is constantly in, but keeping it orderly will help when completing large projects. The hardest part with a workshop is finding homes for large items. If you're a woodworker, you'll have tons of wood you need to store and all the tools that need to be put away when not in use. While these creative spaces don't need to be perfect, they should have some order for you to be able to thrive in.

TIDYING UP

WHERE YOU WORK

WORKSPACE GOALS

1. Set up a workflow that enhances function and focus.
2. Create systems that are visual reminders to handle piles.
3. Find ways to eliminate paper clutter.

PRODUCT LIST

- Desk with storage
- Storage drawer set
- Shallow baskets/trays
- Large basket
- Magazine file holders
- Cord management clips and sleeves
- Decor items
- Label maker
- Label tape
- Shredder

Workspace Tip #1

CREATE A FLOW THAT PROMOTES FOCUS AND FUNCTION.

No matter where your workspace is located or what type of work you do there, the main goal is to get your work done in a timely manner. So think through your daily rhythms and ideal workflow when setting up the space. Arrange your office in the way that allows for the most ease. For instance, don't put your printer on the other side of the room if you constantly print stuff out. Place it next to your desk. Keep office supplies, reference materials, charging cords, and things like that nearby. Aim for the highest efficiency. That's music to any boss's ears!

Workspace Tip #2

DECLUTTER ON THE DAILY.

At the beginning of the day, set aside time to go through your email and trash the junk immediately. Do the same thing for your computer desktop; save and file anything that's needed and trash what's useless. Even though this is tech, the visual clutter and to-dos can be overstimulating and make it challenging to get into the work at hand.

When work is done for the day, declutter your work zone by putting everything back in its place. This means filing paperwork, putting those files away, shredding sensitive papers, placing pens and pencils into holders, and emptying the trash. This will set you up to get started right away the next day. Keeping up with these decluttering tasks at the start and end of each workday will go a long way toward protecting your future self.

Workspace Tip #3

FACE YOUR DESK OUTWARD.

When we walk into a home office, more often than not, the desk is placed against one of the walls, meaning the person's back faces the door. Now maybe you think this allows you to get the most out of the floor space, but what a boring view! Particularly if you have a room that's solely used as an office, try pulling the desk away from the wall and flipping it around to face the room. Doesn't that just sound like it would be a more enjoyable spot to sit every day? And you won't really lose any storage space with this change because you can place other must-have items, like a file cabinet or a printer, behind you. Having these things at arm's length, rather than across the room, is more efficient. If you are in a shared space like a bonus room or playroom, still consider rotating your desk to face the center of the room. While not ideal for focusing, it does allow you to keep eyes on the kiddos while you work. Also, it looks appealing!

Workspace Tip #4

CHOOSE A DESK WITH ADEQUATE STORAGE.

A streamlined, modern desk is so beautiful and popular in home offices. We *love* the look of them, but they *seriously* lack storage space. Work zones can require a lot of little things: tape, scissors, staplers, paper clips, sticky notes, paper, and so on. If you don't have built-in storage, the desktop will quickly turn into a catchall for everything from supplies to that ever-growing pile of papers.

We recommend using a desk with at least three drawers so every little pen and pencil has a happy home. Alternatively, you can always bring in a small drawer set to place under or next to your desk. The key is making sure you have storage for all the essentials. This allows you to eliminate visual clutter and maintain a tidy workspace. We want you to walk into the space and feel ready to tackle the day instead of feeling overwhelmed.

Workspace Tip #5

USE SHALLOW BASKETS TO STORE TO-DOS.

To-do tasks tend to pile up in work zones. All those personal administrative chores—like bills, permission slips, car registrations, insurance cards, and jury duty reminders—need somewhere to go! To keep these to-dos from becoming overwhelming, we suggest bringing in a few shallow trays or baskets for your desk. Create one urgent to-do basket for the time-sensitive tasks, like permission slips, bills, and registration forms. Then create one general to-do basket for everything else.

But we aren't kidding when we say *shallow* baskets. We don't want anything getting buried or forgotten in a deep pile. Having a lapsed car registration is no fun! The goal here is to empty the urgent to-do basket daily and the general to-do basket weekly. If one of the baskets starts to overflow before your designated time to go through it, you know what to do! This system creates a visual reminder to manage paperwork *before* it becomes a problem.

Workspace Tip #6

CREATE A ZONE FOR RETURNS.

Almost every home these days has a pile of returns—that's just the nature of our current culture and online shopping. So it's important to create a designated drop zone for these items.

Use a basket so there's a distinct visual boundary for the items. We don't want them just lying around on the floor or on a shelf or on your desk. The benefit to a system like this is that when the basket is full, you can simply take the entire basket to make the returns all at once. If you see the pile growing, schedule time to make your returns soon. The goal is to avoid a heaping pile because that's when motivation wanes from the sheer size of the task.

Workspace Tip #7

DESIGNATE A MAGAZINE FILE HOLDER FOR EACH FAMILY MEMBER.

As with general papers, the home office is an easy default catchall area for family mementos. This makes sense. You empty out your kids' take-home folders and find an award or piece of artwork to keep. But instead of filing it away with mementos, you set it on the desk to handle later because it's time to get to school. Soon enough, these sentimental items start to pile up. The same happens with birthday or anniversary cards that you want to keep—they get piled on the desk to deal with later.

Just like with returns, create a streamlined habit to make this put-away process more functional. Designate one magazine holder for each family member. Be sure to add each person's name to their holder. Whenever there's something you want to keep, just tuck it into their file. When you open a sweet card from your partner, stick it in the file. The key to this system is that when the files get full, it's time to sort through and move them to the designated memento spot in your home (see chapter 10).

As you can tell by now, keeping a tidy home is *all* about creating realistic systems. We know we're not going to walk upstairs to our kids' memento bin each time we want to save a drawing they did. Implement systems that actually work for the flow and layout of your home. Your goal is to establish systems that are doable *and* maintainable.

Workspace Tip #8

TOSS IRRELEVANT PAPERS RIGHT AWAY.

Done! Unfortunately, if managing paperwork were actually easy, it wouldn't be such a problem for so many of us. Papers accumulate faster than anything else in the home. Even in this digital age, the amount of physical paperwork that stacks up is astounding. If you don't handle the papers quickly, it can quickly feel like you're drowning.

After you get the mail, sort through and toss any irrelevant paper into the recycling bin right away, even before it makes it inside your home. Repeat the same process for your child's backpack. Each night, go through backpacks and immediately pitch the stuff they don't need into the recycling bin. For any flyers with pertinent information, snap a picture with your phone or add it to the calendar right then and there; then immediately recycle the paper.

The overall goal is to minimize the amount of paperwork entering your home in the first place. So switch as many bills and notifications to digital as you can so they arrive via text or email. The less paper that makes it in, the better off you'll be in managing it!

Workspace Tip #9

ADD CORD CONTROL.

If you've worked hard to get your office or workspace tidy and under control, the last thing you want to deal with is a tangled mess of cords. But this space usually has a fair share of electronic equipment, from computers to laptops to tablets to printers to monitors and more. That's a lot of cords around your desk! Our mom, for example, has an office setup that looks like she could work at NASA. *So many screens!* But she has a lovely desk layout with cord management and, most important, she feels good in her space and can get her work done. While there's no way around having them, a few methods can help cords blend in and be a little less intrusive.

First, run cord sleeves along the bottom and side of your desk, then plug them into the wall. Not only does this keep the cords contained, but it's safer for small children and pets. Then, use adhesive clips on the top of your desk to keep charging cords easily accessible. This makes it so much better than digging around under your desk to locate the right one when your phone is dying! Make sure you keep cords at your desk only for objects that are actively and regularly in use. Store your extra cords and cables in a labeled bin in your laundry room. You'll want to keep this system clear and simple because you'll need access to these cords often, so keep only what you need.

LEVEL UP WHERE YOU WORK

Bring in fun decor. Personalizing your office space is an easy way to create a welcoming environment, one where you want to get to work. Adding a few decorative items to the workspace goes a long way in improving motivation and increasing satisfaction. It helps with tidying up as well, since you want *those* items, not your clutter, to be on display.

We suggest finding a few art pieces to put on the walls, ones that you love to look at and that make you happy. If you get cold often, bring in a cozy throw blanket. Do your feet rest on a cold floor? Add a cute under-desk ottoman. These items will foster joy and comfort in an otherwise utilitarian area. Think about small changes that would make your workday more pleasant. You want this space to feel like you and for the room to make you want to enter—and *really* get to work.

SQUARE FOOTAGE PROBLEMS?

Use your walls. Furniture designers know that many people work from home these days and need more functionality, especially in small spaces. There are so many slimline desks out there with drawers *and* storage above. The principle from other areas of the home applies here too: Use vertical space! Use the wall behind your desk to add shelves or pegboards with hanging organizers for storing items (papers, office supplies, reference books, and so on) that might otherwise live on top of your desk.

MANTRA

A tidy workspace will bring a smile to your face.

Chapter Nine

TIDYING UP YOUR GARAGE

Garages can be the craziest places. We've seen garages that hold everything from a great-aunt's couch to dried chicken feet to mountains of recycling. From fishing waders to holiday decor to car seats and strollers for each child. We never know what we'll find when we walk into someone's garage!

Most of our clients have two-car garages, even though only one of the cars can fit inside. Some can't park a car inside at all, because the entire space is being used as storage—and not always by choice. Ready to change that?

Tidying up your garage can be a major challenge because it's another one of those catchall spaces—except here, it's for the *big* stuff. Tools, lawn care items, holiday decor, back stock, ride-on toys, sporting equipment—you get the idea. There's a lot to organize here, and if you're not careful, it can become a mess—standing in the

> **An organized garage is key for those of us who want more ease in our everyday lives.**

way of all your hobbies and holidays and weekend plans. An organized garage is key for those of us who want more ease in our everyday lives.

If you don't have a garage, just imagine that every time we say garage we're saying basement, storage unit, shed—wherever you keep all that big stuff you don't want in the living space proper. These principles all apply!

DECIDING WHAT WORKS FOR YOU

The main goal with garages, as with so many of our other spaces, is to first decide how you want the space to be used. Do you want (or need) it for storage? Do you want to be able to park two cars inside? The answers to those questions will determine the choices you make about what to keep in there.

If your garage functions primarily as a storage space and you don't plan on parking your car in there, we're fine with that! But we still want to help you tidy up this space so everything you have and need is organized and easy to find. No matter how you use the garage, you deserve a system that keeps this space tidy, maintainable, and manageable.

To evaluate your garage space, you'll need to know what's most important to you so you can organize the space in a way that makes your most-used items handy and easily accessible. Prioritize what you use most, and deprioritize what you don't need to touch for months or a year at a time.

As you consider what belongs in here, ask yourself:

- Do you handle your own lawn care?
- Based on your family rhythms, do you need this space to store back-stock pantry items or paper goods?
- Do you decorate for the holidays?
- Do you have any outdoor weekend hobbies (sports, tailgating, camping, gardening) that require organization?
- Do you have a lot of tools? How often do you use them?
- Do you have larger kids' toys that won't fit in your house?

The truth is, your garage is doing a lot of work for you and your family. With so many different items for different people with different interests, there's a lot of competition for space here. Getting clear on what matters to each of you in this space will allow you to better tackle this big task.

KEEPING IT SIMPLE AND ACCESSIBLE

Yes, garages store some of our larger practical items, such as tool kits and lawn mowers, that we need for functional reasons

> **There's nothing better than knowing what you need is right where you left it.**

around the house. But they also often hold the key to our favorite family activities. Large kids' items are stored in this space, such as sporting equipment or outdoor toys. Or gardening tools for those of you who love to spend your time growing beautiful flowers or harvesting delicious foods right in your own backyard. Or gear storage for those of you who go camping and spend your downtime outdoors. What if you could create a system where the start of a new sport season or that weekend camping getaway is just a few bins away?

There's nothing better than knowing what you need is right where you left it. This makes all those favorite fun activities accessible in a moment—and creates less of a barrier to enjoying your time off!

KEEPING ANYTHING DOES NOT MEAN *EVERYTHING*

Although you can keep anything here that works for your family's needs, the trick to maintaining a garage is resisting the urge to put *everything* in there. When that space becomes too packed, you start to avoid it and continue using it as a dumping ground. This starts a vicious cycle, and the garage feels too unruly. This becomes a stressor that you just don't need. We want better for you, your garage, and your mental health.

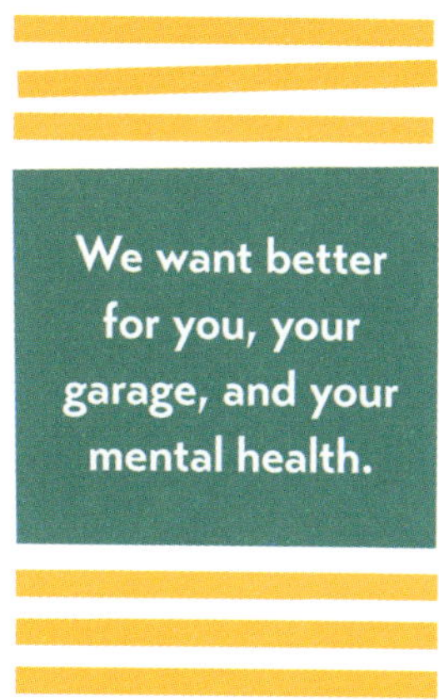

Tidying up your garage *is* a lot of work. But it's definitely possible and so worth it! The best thing you can do is designate bigger chunks of time for you and your partner (or a buddy) to start going through your garage category by category. If you try to tackle it all in a day, it will feel overwhelming pretty quickly. We want you set up for success, so be realistic and plan ahead. Set aside time, then separate things out by category in your mind. When you get to work, begin with one category at a time. In each of your garage-tidying sessions, set a goal to tackle at least one, but possibly two categories. Before long, it'll be the tidy garage of your dreams!

TIDYING UP
YOUR GARAGE

GARAGE GOALS

1. Determine what needs to stay and what needs to leave the garage.
2. Create a layout that makes sense for end use.
3. Rethink some items that could be stored indoors (or donated).

PRODUCT LIST

- Clear lidded bins in various sizes
- Metal shelving units
- Track system for wall storage
- Heavy-duty wall hooks
- Large basket
- Large lidded bins with latches
- Label maker
- Label tape

Garage Tip #1

DETERMINE WHAT NEEDS TO LIVE IN YOUR GARAGE.

If you want to be able to park one, two, or even more cars inside of your garage, you'll need to determine exactly what you want to live in the spaces beside or in between the cars. With the space constraints, you'll need to be picky with what stays and what goes. The categories we hands-down suggest staying in the garage are lawn care tools, pest control, automotive tools, household tools, outdoor play items, camping gear, paint supplies, ladders, and even grilling supplies. Anything else can be stored in another spot inside the home—like the laundry room or attic. The goal is to keep anything in the garage that makes outdoor tasks easier. If an item doesn't fit into that description, it might need to live inside.

Garage Tip #2

CONSIDER THE LAYOUT.

When determining how to plan the layout of your garage, think about when and how you use each object stored there. Once again, the name of the game is ease. You want everything to be stored in the most convenient spot so daily chores and to-dos are less daunting.

For example, store yard tools, outdoor toys, lawn chairs, and in-use strollers at the front of the garage, closest to the main garage door leading outside. Keep your tools, home-repair items, back-stock supplies, and extra refrigerators or freezers closest to the door leading inside. This sensible solution sets you up for success.

Garage Tip #3

REDUCE THE ITEMS STORED IN YOUR GARAGE.

Before beginning to sort your things into categories, it's important to go through what you own and decide if you want to keep, donate, or toss. Remove everything in the garage, and sort it into piles in the driveway. Toss out any old or empty cleaners. Dispose of old sealants and paint cans. Donate any furniture that has sat in the garage for years unused. If you have duplicate home or yard tools, maybe because you've invested in a newer and better version, donate or sell the old one. You really don't need two! We also suggest pulling any memento items out of the garage (see chapter 10) because the weather extremes in this space aren't great for preservation.

Garage Tip #4

MOVE LESS-USED HOME-REPAIR ITEMS TO THE GARAGE.

Store items like pest control or anything potentially hazardous—such as pest control products, paints, oils, cleaners, solvents, or other toxic materials—in the garage. This is also a good place to store large oversized tools, along with any other items you access only on a biweekly or monthly basis.

Garage Tip #5

BRING IN CLEAR LIDDED BINS.

After you have revised down and have only the items you're keeping in your garage, it's time to divide them into categories. Again, like with like! Some examples of garage categories: tape, pest sprays, car wash supplies, gardening tools, sealants, bungee cords, and so on. Making the categories specific is important in a garage space. From yard work to car and home repair to gardening to blowing bubbles with the kids, each of these activities requires specific tools and accessories. Gather the items together and then choose a bin that easily fits them all—but include a little room to grow.

We suggest bringing in an assortment of clear lidded bins in different sizes. In a garage, lids are key! You'll want to be able to stack them to create additional space. Plus, they will keep the contents from getting dusty and grimy. Be sure to add a label to every bin so everyone in the house can easily identify what they need.

Garage Tip #6

ADD METAL SHELVING SYSTEMS.

A main goal with any garage space is getting as much off the ground as possible. This helps with cleanliness as well as using that vertical space to maximize storage. Tall shelves are the perfect spot for all the lidded, labeled bins to live. Line up the bins by category, placing the home-repair bins together, yard care bins together, pest control bins together, and so on. This makes it easy to find exactly what you're looking for.

Another reason to get things off the ground is that a garage can quickly become overrun with pests. Yes, pests. Mice, spiders, and snakes. Oh my! We say "No, thank you" to all of the above. To deter pests from making a home in your garage, use shelving; it will help keep the space clean and clutter-free so you can see what might be trying to make its home on the floor.

Garage Tip #7

USE THE WALL SPACE FOR ADDED STORAGE.

Another great way to get items off the ground is to use the garage walls for additional vertical storage. Most hardware stores offer wall track systems specifically for garages. These wall systems are a great place to store large yard tools like weed wackers and leaf blowers, as well as lighter items like rakes and shovels. You can also bring in heavy-duty wall hooks to hang up things like ladders, wheelbarrows, strollers, bikes, and outdoor chairs.

For hand tool storage, consider adding a peg board to the wall. They're so helpful for grab-and-go access when you need something fast. They're also great if you need someone else to run out to the garage to grab a tool for you, mid-project; they can easily spot it for you.

Overall, anything that can be hung on a wall should be. Remember, the more you move to the perimeter of the room, the more space you have to park your car in the middle!

The easiest starting point is to tidy up your tools with wall space in mind. It's relatively easy to see what the item is and evaluate how often it's used and if there are duplicates. Once you categorize, separate out, and identify what can be donated (anything that you have more than one of), you can organize it all onto wall space or into bins. Follow this process for every category in your garage.

Garage Tip #8

SET UP A ZONE FOR BOXES.

All those cardboard boxes that accumulate in your home? They're the worst, right? Whether it's from day-to-day deliveries or post-Christmas bliss, garages are where cardboard goes to die. We suggest creating a zone for cardboard and any broken-down boxes to be stored until they can be recycled. This zone system will help ensure that your garage doesn't become a home for wayward cardboard and all those cardboard-loving spiders. When the space becomes full, that's your cue that it's time for a recycling run.

Garage Tip #9

MAKE OUTDOOR KIDS' TOYS ACCESSIBLE.

Scooters, balls, bikes, cars, and swim gear—kids' toys are a category that can take up a *lot* of space anywhere, but this is especially true in garages. When it comes to outdoor toys, you'll want them to be easily accessible to little ones. Store them near the outside garage doors and make sure they're on a low shelf. Create a few bins designated for outdoor play with items like sidewalk chalk, bubbles, and Frisbees so kiddos can pull out the whole bin for a fun day outside. We also love to keep a large basket on a lower shelf to store all the different types of balls, making it easy for grab-and-go play.

We like to store adult bikes on hooks on the walls of a garage, but that doesn't work for little kiddos. It's too difficult for them to get the bikes up and down. Instead, tuck bikes into the perimeter of your garage, or if you have a two-plus car garage, line them up in the space between the garage doors. The easier all these items are to access, the more your little ones will be inspired to play. And who among us doesn't love when our kids get off their devices to go outside?

For items rarely used—like bouncy houses, sleds, kayaks—find a spot on a shelf where you can access it when you need it, but that doesn't take up prime, easy-to-grab real estate. And if you haven't used those items in a while, consider donating to free up some storage space.

Garage Tip #10

STORE HOLIDAY DECOR IN CHRONOLOGICAL ORDER.

The garage is a popular spot for holiday decor. Because these items are used only once a year, they don't need to be easily accessible, so we recommend reserving the top shelves for these bins. Divide your decorations by holiday, so all the Easter items together, the Halloween items together, the Christmas items together, and so on. Place each category into its own large bin.

Of course, if you own a large collection of holiday decor, a particular holiday could have more than one bin.

In this case, subdivide your categories. For example, place outdoor lights in one bin, indoor lights in a bin, and tree ornaments in another bin. This will make both decorating and taking it all down much easier.

As you line up your holiday bins on the top row of your shelving unit, another easy but effective tip is to place them in chronological order. So start with Valentine's Day and move to Saint Patrick's Day, then Easter, and so on. This setup will ensure that your holidays don't get mixed together on the shelves and will make it easier to see if you are missing a bin while decorating. Of course, label each bin by the holiday and add any subcategories underneath. For example, one might read: *Christmas: Small Trees, Manger Scene, Stockings*. You can even add the room where it's used if you want a foolproof decorating method!

Garage Tip #11

TUCK SEASONAL ITEMS UP HIGH.

The garage is the perfect spot to store those other seasonal items like camping gear, grilling accessories, gardening tools, and sports equipment since there is no good place inside the home to store them. Use large, lidded bins to store these items by category. Add a label to each bin and tuck them onto a top shelf so they're out of the way during the offseason. When that season comes back around, just pull the bin down to a lower shelf for easy access.

LEVEL UP YOUR GARAGE

Built-ins are a dream. If you really want to level up your garage space, you can design shelving for your walls in the garage. Just like a closet space, you can take all your measurements and preferences to a company that will help you create something unique for you and your family. Because it's easy to run out of space quickly in a garage, maximizing the area with a custom system means you're able to grow with the space over time. Bonus: If you ever go to sell your home, we've found that custom garage shelving is a huge selling point for potential buyers.

SQUARE FOOTAGE PROBLEMS?

Look up. No matter the size of a home, it's easy to run out of space in a garage. Luckily, there are many ways to maximize storage without feeling like the space is overstuffed. Overhead storage systems are available that use the ceiling of the garage as the mounting area, so walls stay simple and streamlined. We use this type of system sparingly since you will need a ladder to access these racks. But this is a great option for small spaces and rarely used items—things like holiday decor, camping gear, and other seasonal items.

MANTRA

What you use the most,

keep it close.

Chapter Ten

TIDYING UP YOUR MEMENTOS

If this chapter title alone causes anxiety, you're not the only one. It evokes the same feeling in us too! Some spaces are truly challenging to tidy up, even for professional organizers. How and where we store our mementos is one of them.

It's simply one area of the home that has a lot of input, little output, and usually isn't well managed or maintained. Not only do people keep their own personal mementos, but they keep things from their children too—and possibly large items (like furniture) or old pictures handed down from parents or grandparents. The amount of tangible "memories" you end up storing in your home can quickly become overwhelming without a functioning system in place.

This is one of those tasks that's tempting to put off. After all, a messy pile of photographs or a tangled box of Grandma's jewelry isn't as urgent as needing to clean a messy kitchen. You tell yourself, "One day, I'll go through it all," and then, sure enough, months and years pass and the pile only grows.

This final chapter is about finding ways to manage and maintain all the special items in your home, both the ones you currently have and the memories that are yet to be made.

WHEN EVERYTHING MEANS EVERYTHING

After I had my son and he became a toddler old enough to hand me rocks and little drawings, I quickly realized I would want to keep every little thing he offered me. I'm pretty sure I still have some dried flowers in my personal keepsake bin from him. We love our babies and their sweet little hearts that fill our homes with random stones and shreds of paper—stuff that means *everything* to them in the moment and, because of that, means everything to us.

Keep anything that reminds you of their personality.

And if you have school-aged kiddos, you already know how much paperwork and artwork comes home with them each day. Though this does eventually wane as they get older, the paper pile is a monster to contain during elementary school. It can be difficult to know what to keep and what to pitch. But, acknowledging that we all love our kids like crazy, let's also agree that we really don't need to keep *everything* they make or every A+ paper they write. Instead, we need to decide on what's *most* important. How can you know? As a rule of thumb, keep anything that reminds you of their personality. When you use this as a filter, it's so much easier to separate out those truly precious "must keep" items from the rest.

FAMILY HAND-ME-DOWNS

Another reason paring down mementos can be difficult is that there's so much sentimentality wrapped up in various items. If you come from a family that values passing down furniture, you know what a (literally) big struggle this can be. Several of our clients have a garage filled with hand-me-downs, not because they *needed* an additional bedroom suite, but because they were *given* one. Most often, they don't really want that king-sized cherry bed frame, but since it was their great-great-great grandma's, they feel guilted into keeping it—even though they have zero intention of using it in their home. This can be tough to navigate.

While we all know none of this stuff can go with us when we leave this earth, many of us still want to honor our loved ones through keeping the things they owned. This is a lovely sentiment, but if we aren't *using* the items from our loved ones, all we really end up doing is becoming a loving storage facility. If you have items that once belonged to family members who have passed on, think

What memory or thing makes you smile and gives you warm feelings for them?

about what really helps you remember this loved one. What memory or thing makes you smile and gives you warm feelings for them? If this table actually evokes warmth for you, then keep it! If not, it may be best to put this in the donation pile. Answering this question is a good starting point for deciding what to keep in your life and what you're ready to pass along.

Sorting through memories is a great exercise to include your children in too. When it's time to go through their closet memento bins, have them look through everything with you and help you make choices on what to keep. This sets them up for maintaining their own memento systems as they get older. It can be a very emotional task for adults and children alike, but by taking small, doable steps, it can be achieved and, might we say, may also be enjoyable!

TIDYING UP
YOUR MEMENTOS

MEMENTO GOALS

1. Create a system for long-term and short-term memento storage.
2. Let go of what no longer stirs your emotions.
3. Find ways to integrate special pieces into your home.

PRODUCT LIST

- Lidded bins in various sizes
- Weatherproof lidded file bin
- Hanging files
- Photo organization case
- Label maker
- Label tape

Memento Tip #1

GATHER ALL MEMENTOS TOGETHER.

The first step to organizing your mementos is identifying how many of them you actually have. Maybe you currently keep some in your bedroom closet, a few in the attic, some in a garage bin, and others on an additional shelf in your basement. When you gather it all in one place, you may be surprised how much you have.

If you've been slowly collecting sentimental items over the years and never taken the time to look through them and consider if they are still important, now is the time. Much of it will likely still conjure feelings of sentimentality and nostalgia, and that's wonderful. But you will likely also be *amazed* by how much of it doesn't mean anything to you anymore. Gathering everything in one spot allows you to take stock of just how much you have, and from there you can evaluate what changes should be made.

Memento Tip #2

GO THROUGH THE COLLECTION ONE ITEM AT A TIME.

Yes, this will take some time. But *you can do it!* It's so worth every minute you spend. If possible, do this in an area far from the main hub of the home. Tidying up your mementos can take anywhere from a few days to a few weeks, so use a spot that can stay a little messy for a while. Consider a guest room or a rarely used corner of the basement, if you have one.

Mementos can be the hardest category to go through because you need time to look at every single thing before deciding whether to keep it. It's an emotional task, so consider breaking it up into small sections over several days or longer. It's just too difficult to plow through these items in a day or two.

Memento Tip #3

BE HONEST AND TOSS.

One of the hardest parts about sorting through mementos is the indecision that comes along with it. People feel like they need to keep every little thing they've collected so they won't lose a single memory. But as you sort through your memories, set aside anything that doesn't hold as much emotion for you anymore. If you look at it and have no clue what it is, toss it or donate it. There's no purpose in holding on to an object for sentimental reasons that has lost its value to you.

And remember: That also holds true for items that were passed down to you by a loved one. For example, if you were given a big box of items that belonged to your grandmother, but nothing in that box *actually* reminds you of her, minus a lamp and a few small plates, don't feel like you have to hold on to all the other items. Keep what you want to keep and ask other family members if they want the other stuff. For any unclaimed items, donate them. They will have a great second life making another family happy!

Other times, you may be tempted to keep an item because you want your children to have it to look back on. But will your child really be upset if you toss out their fifth-grade science report on tree frogs? (*Guilty!*) Please, don't feel obligated to keep everything just because of guilt. Keep what brings you joy, happiness, and fond feelings, and be willing to pass on or toss the rest.

Memento Tip #4

BRING IN BIG BINS.

Instead of having random mementos scattered throughout your home, use bins to store it all. We suggest giving each person in the home at least one large bin labeled with their names. Store those large bins in a central location, like a basement or attic. This is the hub of where all mementos will be stored long-term.

Designating bins for mementos is an easy way to see if the collection is getting out of hand. Seeing it all together, and all the space it takes up, makes decision-making easier. If you've gone up to two or three large bins and all the bins are overflowing, it's time to go through and revise what you're holding on to. That's always the goal: continually making decisions about which sentimental items are worth keeping. The hard truth is, you can either keep the items or keep the space, but you can't have both. Decide what means the most to you.

Memento Tip #5

USE SMALL BINS FOR INCOMING MEMENTOS.

In addition to the memento bins you've just designated for each family member, place a smaller bin inside each family member's closet. Think of the small memento bins as a short-term storage solution for collecting incoming mementos. These smaller bins are for anything you want to quickly tuck away, like drawings, birthday cards, or notes to the tooth fairy. This avoids all those papers piling up on your desk or kitchen counter. You might also consider using a magazine file instead, either on a bookshelf or desktop.

When either the small bin or the magazine file gets full, go through the contents one more time to make sure you still want to keep everything. As you'd imagine, there are usually a handful of items that don't make the cut. What you do want to keep, move into the larger bin to be preserved over your lifetime.

Memento Tip #6

USE FILE BINS FOR SCHOOL MEMORIES.

This is the third bin we recommend creating for each school-aged kiddo. This bin is a lifesaver for parents when it comes to all the school reports, awards, art projects, and report cards that come home throughout the year. Use a weatherproof and lidded plastic file box, which can be found at most retail stores. You want one that can store hanging files. Hang thirteen files, one for each school year starting with kindergarten until twelfth grade, and label each file with the corresponding school year.

With this one bin, you can store your child's entire school career! When they graduate from college and move into their own home, you can gift the bin to them. My kids love to look through their school bins at the start of each school year. I love it too!

Memento Tip #7

BRING IN PHOTO ORGANIZING BOXES.

Physical collections of photographs have started to wane as most people keep their collections digitally. But there's no getting around it—organizing photos can take some time. If you print photos, they can pile up quickly if you don't have a system for them. Most people don't go through them simply because it feels like such an insurmountable task. But it *can* be done, and it's so rewarding at the end.

We suggest compiling all your photos into one place, like a guest room or another minimally used area of the home, so you can spread out. Go into the project knowing it's going to take several weeks or maybe even several months, depending on the number of photos you have and the time you can allot for the project. While this sounds daunting, remember that when it's done in small increments, it's manageable—and it will all get done eventually!

When going through photos, your priority is simply containing and protecting them inside some type of bin. Consider purchasing a plastic photo organizing case. These cases can hold around two thousand photos. They keep the photographs protected because they are BPA- and acid-free, and the case has an airtight latch.

These bins usually come with smaller inner cases so you can categorize your photos while storing them.

After the photos are contained, sort through and organize them by year. If you want to go further, you can also organize by trip, person, and/or month. We love that you can label each smaller inner case, too, which makes finding a particular photo so much easier. Having your photos in one safe spot brings so much peace of mind, and we want that for you.

I went through my personal loose photos a few years ago, and I'm still so proud of myself. Knowing that part of my personal history is "taken care of" makes me feel amazing, like adding a big check mark on my adult to-do list of life! We have worked with several clients on their photos, and every time, this is one of those things that's hard to do but people feel so good afterward.

Efficiency Tip

We think the winter months are a great time to tackle this task because we're often stuck inside our homes due to the colder temperatures and fewer outdoor activities.

Memento Tip #8

FRAME YOUR FAVORITE KIDDO ARTWORK.

We had a client who either traced their kids' handprints or had them handwrite their name on any artwork they kept. Not only were the memories sweet, but so was being able to see how the children's handwriting had changed and how their hands had grown over the years. It was like capturing moments in time. We thought this idea was so sweet! We love the idea of taking this a step further by framing some of these precious memories and hanging them on your walls to enjoy every day.

Memento Tip #9

INTEGRATE SPECIAL ITEMS INTO HOME DECOR.

We want to encourage you to add as many of your special mementos into your regular home decor as possible, without it becoming a cluttered museum dedicated to your kids' art or mementos from deceased family members. If you were given your great-aunt's Fiestaware plates because you also love Fiestaware, add them to your kitchen cabinets. You will love remembering her every time you use them. Maybe you were given a dining room table made by your grandfather. Again, use it! Consider designating a gallery wall to display the art your children have made. You can buy frames that open from the front, which makes switching out the art super simple. You will love seeing it every day, and so will they!

Using these keepsake items in your home will create a feeling of coziness and connectedness for both you and guests. It's a great way to keep memories alive without feeling bogged down by so much stuff. Of course, be mindful. Stay away from using too many keepsakes. You and your family need enough room to breathe, grow, and make your own memories too.

LEVEL UP WHERE YOU STORE MEMENTOS

Customize! This leveling-up tip is for those who tend to keep a lot of mementos or for anyone in the empty-nester season of life. With a little more time on your hands once the kids have flown the nest, you also may have more room in your closets. If you have a good amount of space in an upstairs or guest room closet, create a memento system inside. A contractor or a closet designer can help customize this space with the right-sized slots and cubbies for photo boxes, photo albums, and storage bins. Using a closet for this purpose means that when you're looking for something, you don't need to trek up to your attic and sort through it all. Instead, your favorite memories are always close by.

SQUARE FOOTAGE PROBLEMS?

Use discretion. If you currently live in a smaller place, you already know keeping any extra mementos can be tricky. Obviously, you need to be practical about what to keep. But we still want you to be able to hold on to the things that mean something to you. We suggest keeping a decent-sized storage bin or plastic storage tub up high in a closet. You won't be adding to this every day, so keeping it higher up is okay! Just label it "Mementos" and be discerning with what you add in.

MANTRA

Dedicate a little time now *so later all the*

memories can **shine**

A FINAL NOTE

There's something undeniably satisfying about walking into a home that feels truly *yours*—a place where every item has its place, where clutter doesn't stand in the way of peace, and where every room serves a distinct purpose. Organizing your home isn't just about tidying up; it's about creating a space that nurtures your well-being, supports your goals, and invites calm into your everyday life. Whether you've spent a weekend sorting through the pile of papers on your counter or you've taken months to overhaul your entire home, an overwhelming sense of accomplishment comes with seeing the transformation.

When you step back and admire the organized spaces you've created, it's easy to feel a sense of pride. Not just in the clean countertops or neatly folded T-shirts, but in the journey you've taken to make your space work for you. This is the result of hard work, decision-making, and intentionality. It's a reflection of your values, your focus, and your desire to create harmony in your life. And the best part? That sense of purpose isn't limited to the act of organizing itself—it's something that spreads to every corner of your home, creating an environment where you can thrive.

But the journey doesn't end the moment the last box is donated or the last bin is labeled. Organization is a process that evolves. As life shifts, so too will your needs and routines. You may discover new systems that work even better, or perhaps you'll find that some tweaks are needed to keep the flow of your home in tune with your lifestyle. Over the coming months, give yourself permission to explore, adapt, and refine the systems you've put in place. It's okay to change things as you go—each little change is a part of the journey toward creating a space that brings you joy and supports your ever-changing life.

In the end, home organization is more than a physical transformation; it's an emotional one. The act of creating order in your environment often brings a sense of clarity and peace to your mind. A well-organized home isn't just neat—it feels purposeful. It's a place where you can relax, recharge, and find joy in the simplest moments. So, celebrate your success! Take a moment to appreciate the tranquility you've created. The peace and purpose you've discovered in your home is a well-earned reward, and it's something that will continue to grow as you nurture your space and adapt it to your needs in the months to come.

ACKNOWLEDGMENTS

We couldn't have made this book without the support of our amazing and wonderful partners, Miles and Nick. You both have believed in us from the beginning. Nick, you literally told us to make a book like a hundred times, and we finally asked, "Well how do we do that?!" And Miles, you have known us both since we all had braces and were obsessed with Incubus. Thank you for always being here!

Thank you to all the amazing women (and one man!) we've had the privilege of working with over the years! Each and every one of you has brought such a profound touch to The Tidy Home, and it is forever changed by your presence. Without you, Eleni, we wouldn't have half the laughs that we've had. We found out how it feels to work past midnight countless times, and learned to laugh through the pain. So glad you taught Meg how to use an anchor! To Carli, you may believe in us more than our husbands! Your sweetness and thoughtfulness have changed us and bring so much comfort to our clients. Brooke, sweet Brooke, you keep us in line better than anyone in this world. Your dedication, loyalty, and wit make each day so wonderful. To Delaney and Nick F., we love you both so much. Thank you for everything you've done for us!

Our kids would be so mad if their names weren't in here! Just kidding, we love them all and quite truly we are so thankful for each and every one of you. Thank you for your understanding, your flexibility, and love toward us, especially when we have deadlines. To Levi, Everly, Elliott, Rio, Rue, and Ren—we love you all so much!

And last but not least, thank you to our amazing agent, Carly, and to Harper Celebrate for seeing our vision and bringing it to life better than we could've imagined.

INTRODUCTION

1. Sherri Gordon, "The Connection Between Cleanliness and Mental Health," VeryWellMind.com, updated April 24, 2024, https://www.verywellmind.com/how-mental-health-and-cleaning-are-connected-5097496.

CHAPTER 4: TIDYING UP WHERE YOU GATHER

1. Gordon, "The Connection Between Cleanliness and Mental Health."

CHAPTER 6: TIDYING UP WHERE YOU SLEEP

1. "The Mental Health Benefits of Staying Organized," Anthem, accessed March 5, 2025, https://www.anthemeap.com/sparc/emotional-wellness/mental-health/articles/the-mental-health-benefits-of-staying-organized.

2. Sandstone Care, "Messy Room Depression: 8 Answers About Messiness and Mental Health," Sandstone Care, updated October 27, 2022, https://www.sandstonecare.com/blog/messy-room-depression-8-answers-about-messiness-and-mental-health/#:~:text=Psychologically%2C%20a%20messy%20room%20can%20represent%3A,Trouble%20focusing%20on%20a%20task.
3. Sarah Vanbuskirk, "The Mental Health Benefits of Making Your Bed," VeryWellMind, updated April 3, 2023, https://www.verywellmind.com/mental-health-benefits-of-making-your-bed-5093540.
4. Vanbuskirk, "The Mental Health Benefits of Making Your Bed."
5. Rachel Jones, "The Clutter-Depression-Anxiety Cycle: How to Stop It," Nourishing Minimalism, May 26, 2023, https://nourishingminimalism.com/clutter-depression-and-anxiety-a-vicious-cycle/.
6. Jones, "The Clutter-Depression-Anxiety Cycle."

CHAPTER 8: TIDYING UP WHERE YOU WORK

1. "How Your Workspace Can Support Your Mental Wellness," Calm, accessed March 5, 2025, https://business.calm.com/resources/blog/how-your-workspace-can-support-your-mental-wellness/.

ABOUT *the* AUTHORS

Ea Fuqua is a quintessential older sister and type A perfectionist. She's always craved order and calm in her life while also enjoying many creative outlets. When she became a mother and began juggling a full-time, work-from-home job, the importance of organization and tidiness became so much more apparent to her. She needed order to thrive each and every day!

In 2019 Ea pondered starting a business with her sister and quickly realized what they were both very good at: organization. Once Meg was on board, they never looked back. They were ready to bring peace and calm to other families who were struggling to achieve order in their homes.

The Tidy Home quickly built a loyal following on social media, managed by Ea, who now posts daily to nearly 320,000 followers across Facebook, Instagram, and TikTok. She also handles all partnerships, collaborations, and sponsored content to keep building The Tidy Home brand.

Ever since **Meg DeLong** was a kid, she's created art: from drawing with her dad at five years old, to studying art in college. Leaning heavily into design and visualization, spatial awareness has become a guiding principle for Meg in both her life and business. Now, Meg is a creative entrepreneur, ready for new challenges and experiences wherever she goes.

Meg handles client management for The Tidy Home, designing each project with a focus on the individuals' needs and wants. Meg is also in charge of leading contractors in executing each project to the top of their abilities and creating the best environment possible for each client.

Since 2019 The Tidy Home has worked in hundreds of homes and helped countless individuals get tidy. Starting The Tidy Home Nashville with Ea has been a very exciting adventure that's brought so much knowledge and wisdom to Meg's life.

Be sure to visit our website and socials to learn more and to also find shopping lists for the items we've recommended.

www.thetidyhomenashville.com
@thetidyhomenashville